Digital Participation and Collaboration in Architectural Design

The emergence of new digital and visualisation technologies in recent years has led to rapid changes in the field of architecture. Current drives to incorporate building information modelling as a part of architectural design are giving way to the increased use of IT and visualisation in architectural design, user participation and group collaboration.

As digital methods become more mainstream, *Digital Participation and Collaboration in Architectural Design* provides an accessible and engaging introduction to this emerging subject. Supported by selected examples from research and practice, the book offers an overview of theories, techniques and approaches which readers can apply in their own work. In doing so, it shows how these techniques can influence communication, debate and understanding and encourages readers to see familiar buildings from original and unusual perspectives.

An ideal starting point for anyone interested in the application of digital techniques, the book will help students and professionals in architectural design and digital architecture to understand and embrace new technologies.

Richard Laing (PhD MRICS) is Professor of Built Environment Visualisation at Robert Gordon University, where his research has concerned the use and effects of visualisation within architecture, construction and public engagement. His work has included numerous projects with colleagues from across Europe, as well as the supervision of research students in fields such as collaborative design, environmental economics and built heritage conservation. He was born in Vancouver and grew up in Scotland.

Digital Participation and Collaboration in Architectural Design

RICHARD LAING

LONDON AND NEW YORK

First published 2019
by Routledge
2 Park Square, Milton Park, Abingdon, Oxon OX14 4RN

and by Routledge
711 Third Avenue, New York, NY 10017

Routledge is an imprint of the Taylor & Francis Group, an informa business

© 2019 Richard Laing

The right of Richard Laing to be identified as author of this work has been asserted by him in accordance with sections 77 and 78 of the Copyright, Designs and Patents Act 1988.

All rights reserved. No part of this book may be reprinted or reproduced or utilised in any form or by any electronic, mechanical, or other means, now known or hereafter invented, including photocopying and recording, or in any information storage or retrieval system, without permission in writing from the publishers.

Trademark notice: Product or corporate names may be trademarks or registered trademarks, and are used only for identification and explanation without intent to infringe.

British Library Cataloguing-in-Publication Data
A catalogue record for this book is available from the British Library

Library of Congress Cataloging-in-Publication Data
A catalog record for this title has been requested

ISBN: 978-1-138-06264-1 (hbk)
ISBN: 978-1-138-06266-5 (pbk)
ISBN: 978-1-315-16148-8 (ebk)

Typeset in Univers
by Keystroke, Neville Lodge, Tettenhall, Wolverhampton

This book is dedicated to Audrey, Adam and Abigail.

Contents

	Preface	ix
	Acknowledgements	xiii
1	**Introduction**	**1**
	Summary	9
2	**Digital technologies in architectural design**	**11**
	Key developments in information visualisation	12
	The march to Moscow	12
	John Snow and the 1854 cholera epidemic	13
	Harry Beck	14
	Visualisation in architectural design	16
	Early uses of digital drawing in architecture	21
	Drawing interfaces – drawing, collaboration, communication	24
	The design team	27
	Resistance to the use of digital technologies and the importance of drawing	29
	Drawing as a design and communication tool	30
	Development of ideas through simulation	35
	Information visualisation within education	35
	Usability	40
	Understanding elementary perception-cognition tasks	41
	Prior knowledge	42
	Aesthetics	42
	Summary	45
3	**Digital visualisation in practice**	**47**
	Collaborative working – the digital studio	47
	Collaborative working – online and distant communication	49
	Ideas generation through collaboration	52
	Summary	54

4	**Democratic visualisation**	**55**
	Methods	56
	Democratic access to technology	61
	Summary	70
5	**Collaboration and participation**	**73**
	Democratic engagement in planning and design	80
	Image manipulation	81
	Viewing and rating images online	83
	Greenspace – 'real' growth and connections with social science	91
	Image sorting	96
	Heritage studies	98
	Digital visualisation in architectural marketing ('true grit')	101
	Summary	107
6	**Future directions**	**109**
	Smart cities and architecture	111
	Representation though collaborative devices	121
	Gaming	122
	Citizen engagement	126
	Summary	127
7	**Final remarks**	**129**
	References	133
	Index	143

Preface

Much of my own research in the past few years has explored the development of ways to encourage discussion and debate about our cities and town centres. This has touched on subjects such as how we travel, urban tourism, public space and building conservation, and has often used innovative ways to record or present 'scenes' or environments. One of the central considerations within that work has been the notion that using approaches from digital visualisation to present these environments and scenarios could help people to discuss architecture, and to look at what may be very familiar buildings, or unfamiliar topics, from an original or unusual perspective.

A key challenge within the architectural disciplines[1] in the coming years will be to find ways to encourage everyone to embrace such technology, whilst ensuring that there is a clear intention behind its use to communicate ideas. If we wish to use digital visualisation to encourage debate, then this requires consideration of questions such as 'what is the purpose of a debate?', 'who should be involved?' and 'how can this best take place?' As a consequence of this, practical approaches taken when trying to 'sell' an idea to stakeholders or society, or gain planning consent, may also be entirely different. The book deals with these issues through the use of language and examples which are accessible to a wide audience, with academically referenced discussion, and through a structured and positively critical description of selected case studies.

As mentioned above, the emergence of new digital and visualisation technologies in recent years has propelled the architecture and construction industries into a period of rapid change. This will mean that extensive parts of the built environment may be represented to professional expert groups, and to the wider population, through a complex range of techniques and formats, and issues such as accessibility and usability of the technology and communication methods will become incredibly important.

Preface

It is intended that the book will serve to stimulate debate within the industry, as well as satisfying a wider readership interested in the application of visually arresting digital techniques. Within the industry itself, one need look no further than the rapid uptake of building information modelling (BIM), within which the digital representation of new and to some extent existing architecture is central. Outside of the construction industry, there is a widespread and active community exploring the use of accessible visualisation technologies to allow them to digitally capture and represent their own environments.

By exploring the motivations for using digital visualisation, as well as the application of the methods themselves, the book serves to bridge a gap between technological assessment of visualisation and architecture and concerns regarding how best to communicate architecture both to and between different groups.

My own personal motivation for writing this book stems from many years of applied research dealing with participation in architectural design and involving the use of innovative visual and digital techniques. Those studies at their heart often had research questions arising from study of the built environment (e.g. planning, behaviour of citizens, urban connectivity),

Figure 0.1
Public consultation session using laser scanning.
(Photo taken by author.)

wherein visualisation was employed to facilitate the deeper participation of people in the studies. This experience persuaded me that the techniques themselves often hold a deep fascination for end users but that there is a corresponding requirement to understand how they can influence communication, debate and understanding.

Furthermore, it has become apparent through the development of digital technologies in the past two decades that being able to attach information to models is important and valuable, and that a means to then discuss such information among members of a design 'team' is also important and valuable. Some of the case study examples provided which used visualisation in 'public participation' work were limited by the fact that it was difficult to develop models which had any kind of association with important data. This meant, for example, that an object in a 'scene' (such as a building or a monument) might well have 'looked' like the actual object in real life but making any underlying association was difficult. The development of architectural and geographical software has eased the making of this association over the years, in that files and approaches are now more interoperable and comparable, but this then opens a wider and more fundamental question about who might actually wish to access data, and for what purpose? In any case, if we spend time and resources adding information to a model, who is to say in 10 or 20 years that anybody will actually be able to access and make sense of the information? This practical, and behavioural, aspect of collaboration is discussed in the book, especially in relation to current agendas which seek to provide technical ways in which information can be shared to help collaboration in design, in user engagement and through the life cycle of a building. Technical opportunities exist to support collaboration and engagement, but they require commitment and behavioural changes in order to be successful in practice.

Finally, the book is also intended as a starting point, and to that end contains numerous references to the work of others. Some of the earlier references (Cullen 1961, Eastman 1974, Hornsby 1992) are interesting in that they proposed theories or frameworks to guide future work, but often in the absence of suitable technology which might shape those developments. Although recent professional and academic work within architecture and construction has expended considerable effort on attempting to similarly frame the implementation of BIM (Succar 2009), many of the underlying problems of the industry cannot be solved through technology alone:

- Why should (and could) we engage better with end users?
- Can the problem of inter-team collaboration be solved through the provision of technology?

The reader is encouraged to explore some of these wider texts, as they suggest that the landscape within which we engage with participation and collaboration is one which demands understanding and exploration of both social and technical issues.

Note

1. I am intentionally inclusive in the use of this term, and I refer to disciplines concerned with the design, construction, production and management of the constructed environment, as opposed to being limited to any one particular professional discipline.

Acknowledgements

I would like to give special thanks to the many colleagues with whom I have enjoyed and valued years of discussion, friendship and laughs.

Chapter 1

Introduction

The themes of participation and collaboration are related and share many characteristics. This chapter introduces some of the key concepts, including the notion that participation of end users in architectural design can exist across a range of activities, but to ascend the 'ladder of participation' requires planning and support. The subject of collaboration, particularly within design teams, is introduced.

The themes of collaboration and digitisation in architecture have been prevalent and debated in the industry for decades. Until recently, though, the themes have tended to develop and be enacted through separate activities, studies and initiatives. Therefore, an attempt to trace the lines of either academic or industry study of the themes might identify research following quite discrete paths, for example:

- collaboration within construction teams
- collaboration within architectural design teams
- membership and operation of design teams
- participation of end users and other stakeholders
- the impact of digital technology on design
- the impact of digitisation on construction and technical processes.

One could argue that this lack of connection between the study of collaboration and that of digitisation has been at least in part due to there being a lack of technological (digital) support for collaborative working. On the other hand, an important and pressing observation is that software developers will typically concentrate on the provision of software which is demanded by an industry, thus suggesting that a need for software to support collaboration and participation will be likely to emerge from such practice in a non-digital setting.

Throughout the book, a conscious attempt has been made to illustrate some key examples of connections which can usefully be drawn between digitisation, wide participation (in terms of participants) and collaboration within design. The book recognises, of course, that the participation of end users requires quite different consideration to that of collaboration among members of the design team.

The notion of participation first requires us to think deeply about who we mean by the end user, in that this could refer to people who will eventually live in, nearby or simply experience architecture through their daily lives. Particularly when we consider prominent examples of architecture, the notion of the end user becomes even wider, and people may find value in or have strong opinions about that architecture, and feel that somehow affects their lives, even if they do not use the architecture in any of the above respects.

With regard to collaboration, the topic was the central theme of key reports in the 1990s (Latham 1994, Egan 1998), which highlighted a lack of collaboration and cross-discipline working across the industry, leading to a lack of efficiency and productivity. This has in time seen government and professional body interventions attempting to address this point, often against a backdrop of shifting influences across the design team. The industry has been defined historically by the production of unique products ('every building is different'), often with a new 'team' for each project. Therefore, an analogy with other forms of production (e.g. factory-based car manufacturing) can be misleading in terms of product but relevant in terms of the significant change of mindset required when migrating to a model of industrialised production (Kristensen 2011).

Against a similar time period, we have seen the emergence of digital technologies within the architectural and built environment disciplines. Initially, these tended to focus on the replacement of traditional analogue processes with digital alternatives, most obviously through the substitution of drawing boards with on-screen drawing and electronic tablets to support sketching. Whilst we can discuss the ways in which this process could still be regarded as 'manual', through the use of haptic sketch pads, or simply through the use of a keyboard and mouse in lieu of a pencil or pen, early approaches to digitisation were visual and produced models which did not in themselves contain information beyond visual representation. It is also worth noting at this stage, and we will return to this point, that the interface and methods through which the design team produce drawn material in a digital setting are significantly different from those for generating ideas and producing materials through the use of pen and paper.

Introduction

Figure 1.1
Decision
making through
sketching.
(Image
produced by
Dr Marianthi
Leon.)

Collaboration was possible through sharing of drawings produced by such early digital drawing systems (via email, of images lacking data), but technology had not, in the 1990s, reached a point where it was yet possible, or at the very least easy, to share the models themselves, or to have teams collaborate on their production. Although discussion of the practicalities of building information modelling (BIM) can be traced back at least to the 1980s, the digital modelling software used most widely in the industry prior to the early 2000s tended to be based on the geometrical shapes used to represent a building, rather than the relationships between objects, materials, cost and so on. That is, the model might 'look' like it contains a floor, but users of the model would be unable to use data contained within it to determine if the floor was too large, small, unsupported, or whether it also appeared in drawings and models being used by the architect, engineer, surveyor and technologist. In 1988, with the publication in the UK of a new Standard Method of Measurement (SMM7), came an early attempt to coordinate the production and coding of project information (Coordinated Project Information). Although this was difficult to mandate across all disciplines, and harder still to benefit from in practical sharing of digital data, the seeds of what eventually became a standard approach to coding the components of a building project (Uniclass) had been sown.[1]

At that point, however, various strands of digital innovation had yet to combine in ways which assisted with meaningful collaboration. Drawings (often two-dimensional) produced by the architectural team were not easily compatible with the parametric approached taken by structural engineers, and the production of surveyed measured quantities was still a largely manual and separate process. Furthermore, the oft-cited 'design team' had no mechanism (not a digitally assisted one, anyway) to collaborate, and certainly nothing which placed the models themselves at the centre of collaboration (in much the same way that participants might discuss printed drawings, sketches or site photographs).

The ways in which this situation continued to evolve form one of the core themes of this book, including discussion and elaboration on how the nature of digital participation and collaboration is now closely linked to sharing of data. Whether this extends to encompassing a wider understanding of 'collaboration' is debatable, and worth exploring. It is also important to think about the ways in which we can understand the characteristics of participation and collaboration themselves, and who the parties involved might be.

In order to do this, it is important for us to first understand how the notions of participation in design (or any process involving a wide constituency) can be conceptualised. In her seminal 1969 paper, Arnstein (1969) proposed a 'ladder of citizen participation', with the 'rungs' as follows:

1. citizen control
2. delegated power
3. partnership
4. placation
5. consultation
6. informing
7. therapy
8. manipulation.

We can immediately recognise that the bottom few rungs (up to 'informing') are prominent and established within architecture, and the desire to inform members of the public about the visual impact of new developments would take place almost routinely. However, this might typically occur without a mechanism to transparently (or otherwise) gather information about opinion, or to invite further suggestion. As we move up the ladder, and arrive at 'consultation' and 'placation', we start to think about asking end users or wider constituencies what they might think about a particular planned activity. Where this does not take place in a manner which is combined with deeper forms of participation, however, the activity would offer 'no assurance that citizen concerns will be taken into account' (Arnstein 1969). Methods of consultation might include attitude surveys and wide-invitation public meetings.

Arnstein's example of 'placation' comes with the wry suggestion 'to place a few hand picked "worthy" poor on boards of Community Action Agencies or on public bodies', and brings the valid observation that, without real power or an ability to seriously influence voting patterns and outcomes, the actual influence of such participants is seriously limited. At the top of the ladder, we begin to think about genuine transfer of power to constituents, and an ability for outcomes to be influenced through a structured and meaningful participation process. Through the course of the book, we will consider practical ways in which the use of digital tools has been useful to support such activity. We will also consider, though, the dangers which can come with a blurring of responsibilities and skills, in that we should be careful to avoid asking those engaging in a participation exercise to take on design tasks in which they are inexperienced. The development of a much deeper design brief, and the facilitation of ways in which participants can engage with design throughout a process, though, intuitively bring benefits to the process as a whole.

Likewise, the subject of collaboration and collaborative practice is one which has become a key theme for debate within the industry in recent years, but perhaps for reasons which were not anticipated by many during the 1990s. At that time, a number of reports (Latham 1994, Egan 1998) identified (a lack of) collaboration within professional design and construction teams as being a serious impediment to realising development, efficiencies and industrialisation in the industry. Indeed, one could have argued that the dominance of procurement methods which excluded the partner with most knowledge of construction from the design process (i.e. the builder) made little sense, beyond attempting to secure a cheap price. Although a drive on the back of these reports suggested that collaborative practice could be facilitated through education (e.g. cross-discipline educational practice) and changed procurement practice, the advent and widespread adoption of building information modelling has seen a return to the debate regarding collaboration, but often through the lens of using technology as a way to facilitate information sharing. Whether this actually represents *collaboration* in itself is debatable, and is discussed later. Certainly, although some of the early demonstration case studies undertaken in the UK took place in a context of 'no blame' between parties, the ability of BIM software to track and identify who made certain changes to a model, and why, appears to support the opposite view. We return to this subject in Chapter 2 (in particular), where we explore the development of digital tools within design, and consider how the use of object-based and information-rich models can contribute to the deeper and more meaningful adoption of collaborative practice.

Introduction

Figure 1.2
Design team
collaboration.
(Image
produced by
Dr Marianthi
Leon.)

The second key strand in the book concerns the ways in which the use of digitisation in architecture can in itself be regarded as a major step towards a democratisation of planning and design. This includes discussion of the ways in which online forums have become platforms for discussion and debate, with examples which have been instigated by local 'formal' decision makers, designers, building users and interested parties. A fascinating aspect of such online engagement with architectural design has been the often unexpected line of discussion which can emerge through unmoderated debate (through blogging, online forums and social media). One example has been the worldwide prominence of sites dealing with the subject of 'abandoned architecture'. One can see within the discussions themselves, at once, a genuine interest in the sites being explored, but also a wider realisation of the apparent meaning and implications in terms of a sustainable use of resources, a connection between people and buildings, and an engagement with the constructed environment in ways which go well beyond established academic forums and criteria for membership. We can observe citizens participating in debate and discussion of architecture due to personal, social and cultural connections, as opposed to them holding any particular professional or formally 'educated' connection to the subject matter.

In a number of later sections of the book, this notion of democratisation becomes very important. In some of the examples of projects and previous research which are presented, it would certainly be possible to use the visualisations and digital models in much the same way that they are often and typically used within architectural marketing. In such a situation, of course, anybody viewing the images who was not part of either the design team or some wider decision-making team would be unable to exert influence or make contributions which could lead to significant impact on the design itself. Although it may seem obvious to say so, this book will argue that the visualisation and digitisation processes which are being discussed and described carry genuine and quite powerful potential to act as innovative and creative tools of communication, and that communication can go in all directions. Indeed, until quite recently, it was probably the case that most visualisation and 3D modelling work undertaken within architecture and planning was instigated and completed by a formal design team. In the coming years, it is very likely that we will see the development and rolling out of methods of modelling and visualisation which can in fact be undertaken by the 'non-expert', and the results almost seamlessly incorporated within a formal planning and design process. In later chapters, which deal with democratisation and likely future directions of digitisation in architecture, we deal with some of these factors in greater depth, particularly regarding access to technology and the implications of smart cities.

Finally, one important development in recent years has been the emergence of methods through which actual and widespread participation in *digital architecture* has become more accessible, less financially expensive, less dependent on taught expertise and arguably more

Figure 1.3
Output from photography-based modelling (photogrammetry). (Image created by author.)

democratic. This has in some cases taken the form of free online viewing of models prepared by others, methods through which 3D models can be produced from photographs, and less and less expensive routes through which hardware such as laser scanners can be accessed or at least simulated through cheap(er) products and methods. In some ways this represents a challenge for both the industry and wider stakeholders which is rooted in both technical and social foundations.

From a technical perspective, this again connects with the earlier introduced theme of democratisation in digital architecture, in that the cost of technology is likely to continue to decrease, and accessibility to advanced digital technology is likely to widen and become pervasive in the coming years. From a social perspective, during the 1990s when a number of influential industry and government-led policy documents[2] were published arguing for greater attention to be given to collaboration within the industry, the extent to which our lives were to become dominated by an information rich digital environment (the Internet, digital communication, collaboration in the cloud, and so on) was not foreseen by many. Therefore, it is useful to reassess how this wider accessibility and engagement in digital architecture will impact on the way that we work. Some of the examples of applied research which we will consider in later chapters illustrate very well how democratic access to technology can have a significant impact on both the design of the research itself and also the ways in which participants in a study or a design process are actually able to interact and participate.

In many of my own early research studies, for example, although the intention might well have been to somehow ascend the ladder of citizen participation (Arnstein 1969), the reality was that the use of any particular technology (digital modelling, accessing research studies via the Internet, capturing information about existing environments using digital tools) brought with it both opportunities for the particular study and a requirement to consider some unique limitations which might emerge as a direct result of its use. These considerations now extend to the operation of the design team within practice, where experience and expertise in certain technologies will vary considerably, with this variation certainly not being unique to any particular disciplines, and likely to fluctuate even within disciplines themselves. It is probable this will have a lasting impact on how the industry engages with end users, and on the design process itself.

By way of providing some closing remarks to this chapter, I should also say some more about the growth of building information modelling (BIM) within policy, education and practice. It can be argued that the architecture and construction industry is among the last to undergo a digital transformation in terms of methods, education and working practice.

There is of course a historical legacy which can and should be respected (as is the case with most industries and trades), and finding ways to incorporate the benefits of digitisation in the industry whilst continuing to derive greatest value from traditional practice and methods remains a key challenge. One underlying theme which recurs during the course of the book is that of a need to use technology and digitisation when it appears to offer capacity and capability in addition to, and in parallel with, other non-digital techniques. We could also consider this in terms of embedding and integrating digital visualisation as part of the design toolkit. I have been struck in recent years by the extent to which discussions about BIM are often prefaced by what appear to be reassurances to an audience that what is being considered is not in fact about computers, or digitisation, or visualisation at all. This, I would argue, is helpful but to some extent runs the risk of underplaying the centrality of this actually being a process through which working practice, outcomes, the design process and (potentially) the buildings themselves will be supported by and potentially influenced by the use of digital tools.

Some of the examples which I touch upon in this book demonstrate quite clearly that the use of digitisation carries genuine potential to enhance, support and even drive the design process. Other examples which we discuss later in the book (particularly in Chapter 5) deal with wider participation in the design of landscapes and streetscapes. These similarly seek to demonstrate that the processes whereby models can be applied and tested within both research and practice environments benefit from outcomes that are not thematically tied to the digital techniques (e.g. aesthetics, preference studies), but which nevertheless could not have been undertaken in the absence of those tools. Therefore, it is arguably important that we never lose sight of the ultimate goals of any particular project or intervention using new techniques. Where the intention is to enhance collaboration and involvement of a wider design team, any technology which is brought to bear to help support that process must be appropriate and tested in terms of how it assists that process and that intended outcome, as opposed to being an outcome in itself. Where any policy document advocates the use of digitisation to support collaboration or participation, we must either presume or critically assess the extent to which digitisation will actually support and even enhance the former.

Summary

These are themes to which we return throughout the course of this book, and which can be illustrated and evidenced through the use of selected case studies and examples of digitisation, taken from both industry and from applied research. In each case, an effort has been made to indicate what the overarching aim of the study project was at the outset, and to set the use of digitisation within that context.

The theme of collaboration within design teams has grown in prominence, due perhaps to a wider awareness of the benefits which might accrue in terms of efficiencies, design certainty and project outcomes. The subject of user participation in design has been prominent within both research and practice since the 1960s, and we touch upon examples from that research in later chapters.

Notes
1. Further information about Uniclass and Coordinated Project Information (CPI) can be accessed via www.cpic.org.uk (accessed 18 April 2018).
2. Referring again to Latham and Egan.

Chapter 2

Digital technologies in architectural design

The chapter deals with how embedded and emerging digital techniques have been used within architecture, both to help develop ideas in the mind of the 'design team' and then to communicate those ideas to a wider audience. The chapter opens with a wider discussion of information visualisation, in order to make clear the importance of communication, insight and intention within the choice of visualisation method.

This book is concerned with the ways in which digital technologies can be used both to support collaboration between participants in design and to encourage and support participation among groups who might otherwise not be part of a technical or professional team. Later chapters will discuss and explore why these might be desirable goals, and will refer to a whole range of studies where such issues have been investigated. What is important to recognise, though, is that people and engagement are at the heart of this discussion.

A key point when considering any method of visualisation, and particularly visualisation of information, is the result of looking at a diagram, picture or other image (Spence 2007). Where that result has been acquired in the mind of the observer, rather than as a result of text or statistical analysis, we can say that 'insight' has been acquired. The examples in the next section all show how visualisation can be used to illustrate information, and the example of John Snow in particular illustrates how a visually driven approach to understanding a topic led to insights which would have been otherwise unlikely to be derived.

In this sense, we must try to remember that visualisation is essentially a cognitive activity, which is not reliant on computers. Of course, much of this book makes a great deal of the manner in which computers and IT can be used to facilitate the visualisation process. However, we must not confuse this process of visualisation with the aim of the exercise, which is to assist understanding and to identify previously hidden facts. Previous research by a range of authors (for example, Lim et al. 2004, Sener and Wormald 2008) has successfully studied the relationships between designer, medium used to design, and the resultant visualisations. Such studies have shown that the approach taken to visualisation itself can affect the insights drawn, and that care should be taken to match the visualisation method (e.g. sketching, computer-aided design (CAD), 3D modelling, physical modelling, painting, etc.) to the desired and intended purpose of the exercise.

It is also true that by using visualisation we open up the possibility of juxtaposing information of different types on the same image or model. For example, it should be possible to incorporate details of material and construction design with temporal (i.e. time) or environmental data (e.g. temperatures, insulation values, and so on). Spence (2007) suggests that we could also categorise such data in terms of whether it is quantitative (or qualitative), ordinal or categorical, and that we can then aim to draw relationships between these.

Key developments in information visualisation

In recent years, a range of seminal approaches to the visualisation of information have been discussed by researchers within visualisation, information management and HCI (human–computer interaction/interface design). The rationale for this can be attributed to the clear, straightforward and illuminating manner in which data was presented, and the extent to which the visualisation process itself then influenced people's understanding of the underlying data. Whilst the examples presented in this section directly influenced a range of discipline areas, including history, workforce deployment, health studies, urban planning and transport management, all have resonance in the modern world, and can easily be translated to needs within modern architectural design, urban planning, construction and building maintenance.

The march to Moscow

Charles Joseph Minard was map-maker to Napoleon and his illustrative map of Napoleon's 1812 campaign and march on Moscow has become recognised as an important illustration of the manner in which visually straightforward representations of data can be used to convey complex information to the reader.

Minard's map[1] illustrates a disastrous military campaign, where Napoleon started out with 440,000 soldiers and returned with only 10,000. The map successfully conveys the size of the army at various points on the route, the temperatures endured, and ultimately the extent to which the returning army was a tiny fraction of the original. The reader arguably requires little explanation of the difference between the two colours (journey there and back), and the map in itself serves to encourage a retention of information about the campaign in a manner which might be more difficult using traditional text and tables. As Spence (2007) wryly notes, though, 'the map might not be entirely suitable as a recruitment poster'.[2]

A comparison can be easily drawn from how such approaches could be manifest in some typically used approaches to the visual communication of information in construction. For example, the critical path theories often used to display and represent information concerning the order, scale and timing of construction tasks take a heavily simplified approach to communication, which, although visually distinct from images of 'actual' construction, do well to successfully convey complex relationships between tasks and resources.

John Snow and the 1854 cholera epidemic

A particularly interesting example of information visualisation, from the field of health studies, concerns the well-known outbreak of cholera in London in 1854. At the time of the outbreak, it was generally thought that cholera was spread through the air, or through person to person contact. Although there was little or no medical evidence to support that theory, the response of authorities at the time had been to encourage those suffering to be kept apart from healthy individuals, although this had little apparent effect on the spread of the disease.

Nowadays we are, of course, well aware that cholera is spread through contaminated water supplies, a fact which was made apparent through the visual analytical work of Dr John Snow. Snow mapped the incidence of outbreaks against various physical features within the streets most badly affected, and noted that infections appeared to be concentrated around outside water pumps, used by local residents to supply water for drinking. Snow hypothesised that there was a link between the water supply and the outbreak, and closing off the pumps led to an immediate and very significant drop in the rate of infection. That such a breakthrough was possible in the absence of modern techniques enabling chemical analysis of the supply can be attributed solely to the use of a visualisation technique. Had Snow relied on commonly held medical beliefs of the time, such a breakthrough would almost certainly have gone undiscovered.

Again, it is possible to draw modern parallels with work in the built environment, possibly most notably in relation to the development of

Figure 2.1
John Snow pub, at the site of a water pump in Broadwick Street, Soho, London. (Photo taken by author.)

research concerning workflow and ergonomic design of sites (Osman, Georgy and Ibrahim 2003).

Harry Beck

It is interesting to note that one of the most widely recognised and used examples of design from the 20th century was produced not by a designer, but by the underground electrical engineer Harry Beck. Beck worked as an engineer with the London underground system and recognised

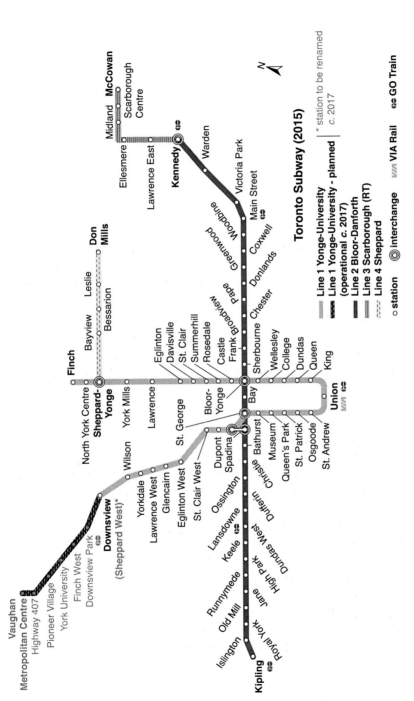

Figure 2.2 Map inspired by Harry Beck's design for London tube map. (https://commons.wikimedia.org/wiki/File:TTCsubwayRTmap-2007.svg)

that users of the system had no real reason to need to know exactly where the actual routes of each train travelled. That is, one can only get on and off trains at stations, so there is no strong transport-related reason to know where the middle of a line might pass under. Early versions of the (pre-Beck) underground map included accurate representations of major streets, and crucially did little to simplify routes for users. Beck's own map made a number of visualisation breakthroughs, including the use of nodes to represent changeover points, and the clear use of colour coded lines to denote each route.

Although the river Thames is shown in an abstract form, the map gives little space to real geographical distance, and some stations which appear on the map to be very close are actually far apart (and vice versa). Beck's map continues to have a huge influence on the way in which most transport systems are represented throughout the world, and its ability to simplify and make clear complex issues of actual transport logistics (e.g. time of travel, ticket purchase) has been drawn on by many organisations to suggest anything from a smooth form of managerial operation to subtly implying to tourists that countries are smaller than they actually are, thus placing readability and transparency of information over geographical realism.

Visualisation in architectural design

Recent research has explored the nature of the design team in construction, and methods through which the multi-disciplinary team can work to collaboratively develop ideas and solutions. This has included discussion of variations in terms of working practice between professions, and how this might differ between practitioners and those still in education (Kokotovich and Dorst 2016, Stompff, Smulders and Henze 2016).

One might argue that the field of digitisation, including visualisation of designs, data, information and so on, requires technical development to sit at its heart. After all, many of the aspirations of the 1980s to somehow coordinate the information contained in projects has only become possible through the iterative development of computer-based systems to allow this to happen. However, one could also contend that the process must be driven by user need, rather than what appears to be technically interesting or challenging. That is, visual methods (sketches, drawings and so on) have been the main form of communication within the industry for centuries, and moves to incorporate digital tools in the design process cannot and should not ignore that point. Where the two can proceed in parallel, perhaps this represents an ideal scenario, yet requires the design team to be able to convey their own creative and working processes, and for these to be understood and acted upon by software and hardware designers.

Traditionally, architects and urban designers have presented design ideas to clients using static representations such as scale plans and sketches. Architects' plans, although accurate in terms of measurement, rarely give the non-expert viewer a 'feel' for what the space will be like when it is finished. It is commonly acknowledged that people often have trouble understanding architects' plans, which can lead to discontent with the end result (Appleyard 1976). As an alternative or additional method of presentation, sketches are often favoured by architects as a method to present ideas in a more fluid style, and are believed to promote feedback and discussion through their 'unfinished' appearance (Schumann et al. 1996).

While plans and sketches are still the most common means of presentation between architect and client, there is a growth in the area of dynamic 3D modelling. Today's student architects, architectural technologists and designers are taught the use of Computer-Aided Architectural Design (CAAD) as a matter of course, and a plethora of new tools have emerged to make it easier and quicker to sketch and finalise a design using computers. As a result, dynamic walk- or fly-throughs of 3D models are becoming more common, enabling viewers to visually experience an as-yet-unbuilt environment. As an extension to this, and perhaps signalling a likely future use of most packages, we normally experience the world via a flow of changing visual images. It can be argued, then, that dynamic presentations of a future environment might be likely to provoke perceptions and reactions closer to those that would be found in the real world than those that would be provoked by static images.

In government and industry drives to encourage and support the adoption of building information modelling (BIM), one is often struck by the extent to which an emphasis is placed on people, and how people work and behave. BIM refers to the use and application of collaboration throughout the life cycle of a building, underpinned by shared 3D models, attached to structured data and information.[3]

Thus, discussion about collaboration through BIM should logically lead naturally to much deeper discussions about collaboration in general, and we return again to the unresolved debate from the 1990s (Latham 1994, Egan 1998). Similarly, discussion about data sharing deals on the one hand with technical ways to share files and information, yet on the other hand the emphasis will very often return to tracing behaviour and liability. Nevertheless, such discussion will usually be topped and tailed with arguments which again draw attention to digitisation of processes and ways of working residing at the heart of a project. This is important and brings us to consider a legacy of digital tools within design, wherein we can discuss the difference between systems which are aimed at supporting design, engagement and participation, as opposed to systems which aim to somehow mimic traditional drawing and representation. Whilst the former can arguably be said to bring new techniques and technologies into play, attempts to replace the pen, paper and suchlike with digital tools require a different perspective and have followed a different narrative and development process.

Whilst it is certainly useful to remind ourselves of a number of trajectories which have been followed by the industry since the 1990s, we must bear in mind that the paths concerning digitisation, collaboration and participation have not necessarily been followed in parallel, or even with great consideration being given to the connections which might exist between them. In the early 1990s (Koutamanis 1993), for example, academic discussion switched to the use of computers for the visual representation of architecture, and the potential to significantly extend the ways in which CAD systems could be used to categorise the components and content of digital models, and the computerisation of design information. Within such research, there was also discussion of the digitisation of material compiled and presented in a non-digital format (sketches, drawings, schedules), and the use of CAD systems to automatically recognise key features and components. One might argue that this remains

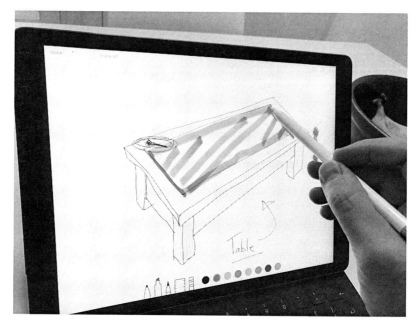

Figure 2.3
Digital sketching.
(Photo taken by author.)

a challenge, albeit one which perhaps affects digital-to-digital recognition (such as in the use of data heavy and highly detailed light detecting and ranging, or LIDAR, point clouds). We also saw discussion (Koutamanis 1993) of the potential for the seamless and planned use of CAD across the design, construction and in-use phases, and again it is useful to reflect on the ways in which this has resonance in the current development and application of BIM.

If we refer to many of the discussions regarding collaboration and collaborative practice which were under way during the 1990s (Pahl, Badke-Schaub and Frankenberger 1999), they rarely if ever find a focus within the realm of digitisation, and they very rarely make reference to the use of such technologies as a route to be followed by the industry as a whole. Nevertheless, as technology has evolved and advanced to the point where we can use digitisation to support collaborative practice, it is the aims of the industry which emerged in the 1990s which again return to the fore and become a guiding light for the future development of that technology. Aspirations of the industry, which can certainly be traced back to the 1980s, to ensure that work is coded and presented using hierarchies and taxonomies easily understood across the industry have now started to finally take hold, given that technology has advanced to the point where these processes can be properly supported (with reference again to the drive for Coordinated Project Information).[4]

Succar (2009) offered a comprehensive contextual analysis of how both academia and the industry should and could view the development of information modelling in the next few years. Various models have been offered of BIM 'maturity', most of which focus upon the extent to which the digital models are shared (individual, through to federated and centralised models), and the ways in which the data could be applied (e.g. during the life cycle). Succar offered an interesting perspective, though, in that his own framework suggested that maturity could develop thus:

- stage 1 – object-based **modelling**
- stage 2 – model-based **collaboration**
- stage 3 – network-based **integration**.

In the sense proposed by this framework, collaboration and learning to collaborate are placed at the centre of the path to be followed, and this represents a key hurdle for the industry to cross. After all, the issues of a lack of collaboration and sharing of information and knowledge across the industry are hardly new (Egan 1998), and tools such as those associated with BIM may not, in fact, have been developed to facilitate deep collaboration, even if they are capable of (technically) allowing and (technically) supporting data sharing.

Another slightly different perspective on how building information modelling might be implemented in practice was presented by Jung and Joo (2011), who concentrated instead on consideration of how digital systems may be implemented across the industry, within individual organisations (for example, constituent members of the design team, the client or the builder). That work also recognised that although industry wide standards may exist, the ways in which these are likely to be implemented and rolled out will depend on managerial issues and policies. This means, in effect and practice, that although the technical problem of being able to share files between various software packages is probably quite easy to solve, using file types and where possible open source file configurations (Industry Foundation Class, IFC), deeper challenge perhaps exists for all participants in the information modelling process when we start to think about the categorisation of data, such as elements and objects.

Succar (2009) tended towards describing collaboration within building information modelling in terms of knowledge and data sharing. This is a useful lens through which to regard the technical practice of BIM, as it allows the collaborative framework to remain focused on the technical capabilities and data sharing characteristics of the three stages (modelling, collaboration and integration), as proposed by the author. 'Knowledge', however, within the context of BIM, tends towards making reference almost exclusively to the information contained within a model, whilst the notion of model-based collaboration is perhaps similarly limited to the consideration of data interchange between various data file formats. Succar rather successfully sets the scene for a particular strand of research exploration, within which we can usefully begin to interrogate some underlying themes. He mentions, for example, the use of visual language within the industry, and a need to explore how this may be developed and tailored to respond to the emerging technical challenges. This is important and relates to later discussion in this book regarding the use of visual media (e.g. sketching) to develop and communicate ideas.

What I would be inclined to argue at this stage is that much of the digitisation we have seen taking place within the industry over the course of a number of decades has either tended to directly replace existing and established traditional, analogue tools or sought simply to somehow augment existing practice. What we have arguably seen much less of has been any significant move towards that digitisation representing a form of industrialisation. What sets the object-based and information-rich modelling we see within BIM to one side of that digitisation trajectory is that the relationships between aesthetic design and technical aspects of the construction process are far closer than at any stage in the past. That is, conceptual ideas within a BIM environment will be data rich, and that data can be carried through to the technical design. However, the nature of many of the software tools commonly used within BIM-enabled design practice means that there is a need to attach technical detail at an early stage, with the implications of those choices being evident.

Added to this we have the capacity for a far wider team of participants to contribute to the design and modelling process. One might be so bold as to argue that an industry which has shown itself to be fairly intransigent with regard to collaborative working within the team, but arguably even more so with regard to the active participation of end users, may find it rather difficult to enact significant behavioural change. Therefore, what Succar identifies as a constraint on the meaningful adoption of BIM in practice, namely social phenomena, requires specific attention. In this chapter, we will touch upon some of the digital tools and techniques which have developed over the years, and which may help to ameliorate this process. In later chapters, we will explore practical studies through which it has been possible to investigate in greater depth the impact of digital tools, and the capabilities of those digital tools, when attempting to foster an environment of open collaboration and participation.

The following sections take us through the development of digitisation from the 1970s, with an emphasis placed on technology to be used by the design team, and where an understanding of what is meant by 'the design team' is perhaps narrower than that which would now be accepted and understood by most in the modern construction industry. We will return in later chapters to the notion of collaboration and participation involving a much wider constituency, including participants from outside of the professional industry (including the general public, building users and other stakeholders). For the moment, though, we will focus our attention on professions within the industry.

Early uses of digital drawing in architecture

Although the early development of Computer-Aided Architectural Design (CAAD) concentrated on the production stages of projects, the potential for using digital media and CAAD at the early design stages has been recognised for many decades (Eastman 1974, Hyde 1989).

Eastman, who would later become a highly influential voice in the development and application of BIM in practice, put forward a number of key arguments in 1974 which still hold resonance today. Arguing, at the time, that the USA lagged behind other countries in terms of the application

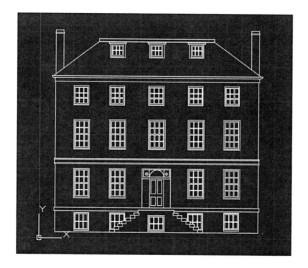

Figure 2.4
Typical CAD output. (Image created by author.)

of CAAD, Eastman explicitly associated the use of computer technology in architecture with the theme of industrialisation. He argued that the dominance of small companies in the industry and a lack of national crises (housing shortage and suchlike) meant that a widespread demand for the revolution of practice had not (as yet) taken place. This was reflected in a relative lack of funding for applied research in the subject area, with the practical application of CAAD being difficult due to the large amount of space and investment required to deal with the hardware and data storage requirements. Three areas of research which were being tackled, and which certainly still hold relevance and importance today, were:

- the digital **representation** of space and objects
- **spatial planning** (using algorithms, in this early discussion) and
- what was described as **man/machine communication** (typically studied within human–computer interaction, or HCI, research in the intervening period).

One could argue that the issue of how to represent and arrange objects in a digital space has seen the greatest advances (model viewing, manipulation). Furthermore, matters such as clash detection have taken a central place in the development of architectural software. Where Eastman's early paper still holds most powerful resonance, though, lies in the discussion of HCI:

- methods and approaches through which we can find meaningful connections between the digital model and drawings, and

- means through which software can make useful interpretations of sketches.

Examples discussed included early digital drawing tools (tablets) and methods through which existing drawn information could be taken into a digital domain (cameras, as opposed to scanners). Whilst this might well have been a basic aspiration in the early development of CAD systems, more recently the move towards models which contain information 'about' objects (beyond their size and appearance) means that there is a need not only to identify basic and 'lower-level' information such as vectors and dimensions, but also to be able to recognise (in drawings produced using traditional methods) the higher-level components and detail contained within (Lu et al. 2005). This again reminds us of the potential for digital models to be used through the life cycle, but also of the fact that digitisation of information will not refer solely to new buildings and new design.

Again, though, Eastman returned to a connection between CAAD, industrialisation and prefabricated building systems as the most obvious route to widespread adoption of such systems, signposting a gap between intellectual demand and technical capability which would not be narrowed until the significant development of CAD/CAM and advanced digital prototyping systems much later.

Complementary research from around the same time (Willey 1976) suggested that there was a need to find connections between traditional approaches to design (such as drawing, physical model making, photo montage, and so on), and that an extension of existing manual techniques (sketching) could drive the development of new digital tools. Willey also described how systems at the time appeared to be geared towards early stages of design, or (and more usually) towards the intensive production of technical design and construction drawings. The centrality of drawing

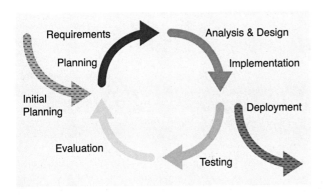

Figure 2.5
Iterative design. (https://commons.wikimedia.org/wiki/File:Iterative_development_model.svg)

as a key part of the design process, as opposed to simply being a medium to express ideas, was highlighted, as was the importance of an interface which complemented the designers' capabilities (rather than driving the process of design *per se*). The work referred at a conceptual level to the automated generation of sketch ideas, a subject we will return to later when considering the place of simulation within recent CAAD and BIM software.

Hyde (1989) argued in favour of following a design process whereby ideas are generated through the iterative use of sketching, and where the design process was supported by both reason and discovery. Through this, discovery could emerge from the design process itself. In terms of graphical problem solving and visual recording, Hyde argued (through observation of paired experiments) that digital means existing at the time were capable of being used to mimic traditional early stage design processes. The argument was also put forward that CAAD systems offered 'inherent potentials' which were quite distinct from traditional non-digital techniques and tools. However, those potentials would not likely be realised if both the development of the systems themselves and the anticipated design processes did not evolve as a consequence. That is, CAAD would only prove to be truly effective where design processes and workflows utilising CAAD developed and evolved to recognise the inherent qualities of the new tools, systems and skills required.

Drawing interfaces – drawing, collaboration, communication

As identified in parts of the preceding discussion, the manner in which a designer and design team are able to interact with a digital system is of vital importance, as the potential to see the system itself leading designs due to a cumbersome or otherwise influential interface is obvious. Research undertaken in the early 2000s (Bilda and Demirkan 2003) identified that some of the benefits of traditional drawing and sketching, including an ability to support perception of 'visual-spatial' features, production of alternative solutions and even understanding of the design problem itself, appeared to dominate when compared with digital modelling tools (that particular study used a CAD interface, with no reported mention of a tablet, or suchlike). We will return to the topic of sketching being useful in design development later, including how this might be effective across groups (Jonson 2005, Van der Lugt 2005). Seminal work from the 1990s (Suwa and Tversky 1997) demonstrated the value of sketching within the design process, and how designers are able to benefit from the ways in which sketching can help to 'crystallise' design ideas at the conceptual stages. With regard to the methods through which designers are able to sketch within a digital domain, it is interesting to consider some of the physical interfaces which were developed during the 1970s and 1980s. What is perhaps most obvious with the benefit of hindsight is that many of these interfaces seemed to be directed towards not exactly the replacement of traditional methods of drawing and sketching, but rather somehow providing a kind of digital surrogate. For example, there was the development of early electronic tablets, presumably in an attempt to avoid requiring artists and designers to interface with design software using the keyboard and mouse. In this sense, some of the immediacy of sketching was preserved, albeit in a form which arguably failed to also mirror the benefits of the rapid iterative design cycles which are possible when using paper and pens.

Some early studies within the field of design recognised the potential value of using tablets and light pens to mimic the sketchpad, with some discussion of speed and ease of use (Davies Cooper and Cooper 1984), although there were limitations in terms of the ability to find connections between the resultant sketches (useful for presentation) and the main CAD files (Tovey 1989).

What is perhaps more interesting, when we consider recent technical developments in terms of the use of digital devices to allow not only two-dimensional sketching but also immersive three-dimensional design work, is the apparent fact that digital tools are now beginning to realise the additional and quite different potential which they offer. We will talk later about the possibility of using digital design methods and their interface with the real physical environment, through the use of CAD/CAM and 3D printing, to bring some kind of logical end point to the early conceptual design stages as well as the development of technical design solutions.

One might argue that this does not actually address an important philosophical point: the inherent and very important connection between early conceptual design sketches and their continued relevance throughout the technical design stages. Within that particular thread of discussion, we are quite overtly recognising that the medium of design can in fact assist, influence and in some cases even drive the outcomes of the design itself. As we noted earlier, it is also true that visual methods of communication have in fact been the dominant means through which design and technical information has tended to be transferred between members of both the design team and the wider construction and building team. In plain terms, the industry as a whole has always communicated using a visual language, whether through sketching, technical detailing or rendered digital models.

It is interesting to consider how the emergence of immersive digital sketching tools might begin to find a place in the mainstream, but it is also important to think about how the prevalent use of such technology might begin to affect the design process and outcomes. One study (Israel et al. 2009) explored how the inherent differences between 2D and 3D sketching can be understood, arguing that the cognitive difficulty of attempting to represent 3D environments on a 2D plane is a challenge to the designer. Of course, one might argue that the education process of most members of the construction design team involves understanding how a 2D drawing (conceptual or technical) is representative of a 3D environment or shape, but the third hypothesis of that study – that the sketching *process* will be influenced by the choice of sketching *medium* – is critical. The results tended to show no benefits to using 3D virtual sketching over 2D sketching/drawing, in terms of creativity and aesthetics. There did appear to be enthusiasm among participants to explore the use of such emerging technology in more depth, though, suggesting perhaps that the approach held potential (at the time, anyway) yet required further development of the interface and tools. Within the context of our discussion, and returning to the theme of collaboration between professionals and with the end users of architecture, we should also consider the ways in which emerging immersive visualisation techniques might be used to support discussion and debate within groups. This strikes one as being important, as the notion of creativity is one which can and should exist not only within the designer, and the wider design team, but which can also extend into a creative application of collaboration and participation in professional practice. Till (2009) refers to the work of Vesely (2004), arguing that 'drawings and other media are seen not as remote abstractions but as the place for the exchange of ideas, information, and inspiration open to all participants in the architectural process'. Till then provides a powerful description of the connections between ideas, narratives and stories, and how these can then translate into or inspire sketches and drawings which will come later in the design process. Elsewhere, Till (2009) draws our attention to the use of drawing and sketching as a central communication medium, not only within architecture but also the construction industry as a whole. In this, we run the risk of presuming that drawings can at once serve a number of purposes, and equally well in each case. For example, if a drawing is effective in terms of representing the aesthetic appearance of the building, could that same drawing or set of drawings be used as part of the production process? Again, we should consider the potential connections which exist between digital design and both CAD/CAM and industrialised production.

Till refers to the apparent ability of drawings to represent architecture in a restrained manner, but nevertheless a manner through which the contingencies of architecture are either suppressed or completely absent. For example, Till refers to a freezing of time through the use of various types of image (sketches, drawings and photographs), yet this notion of freezing time is just one example of how emerging digital tools allow the modeller, and to some extent the use of the model, to play with dimensions and characteristics in a way which was not possible, or at least rather difficult, prior to the advent of the digital era.

Elsewhere (for example, in Ibrahim and Pour Rahimian 2010) one begins to follow an argument where one can see an increasing awareness that tools developed to replicate the visual process of drawing by hand lack the tangible experience of manual drawing and can inhibit the design process as a result (and I would tend to include purely visual 3D digital modelling tools). We begin to see a line of enquiry opening up where the future development of drawings tools and software will be likely to feed off the unique potential of ICT tools:

- simulation (including environmental and performance)
- information modelling and management
- surface forming
- immersion (VR and AR).

Thus, tools are able to act as a significant extension of the existing suite of methods available to the team. The importance of this when we consider the wider design 'team', potentially including members who approach the creative process in a multitude of ways, is clear.

The design team

One theme to which we will return in later chapters is that of the 'design team'. The UK CDM regulations[5] state that a *designer* is 'an organisation or individual whose business involves preparing or modifying designs for construction projects, or arranging for, or instructing, others to do this. Designs include drawings, design details, specifications, bills of quantity and design calculations.'

When we now think again about the content, nature and use of BIM in the industry, it becomes clearer that the design team might well be quite wide in terms of membership and scope, but that this breadth of involvement comes with a need to manage design activities. The formalisation of the notion that all participants in a design process be regarded not only as a member of the team, but also as design participants in their own right, is of great significance, particularly against the backdrop of industry wide collaborative working (including the facility to track the nature of that collaboration using digital tools). Earlier work in the 1990s (Whyte 1999) established that the discipline-specific and almost isolated nature of professional groupings and academic training of the disciplines forming constituents of the design team either can help to foster collaborative practice or could in itself act as an impediment to that collaboration being productive and positive. Whyte also spoke of the need for teams to embrace the group participation method, including an understanding of individual and shared expectations, and the dangers of group dominance by one or more team members. Such an understanding of collaboration and the importance of the need to embrace the idea as well as the practice of group participation and collaboration appears to be crucial, yet requires psychological and behavioural commitment on the part of all those involved. This cannot be created and realised solely through the use of a kind of digital surrogate. That is, *active* participation in a group requires a commitment on the part of the individual (or at least on the part of the company employing that individual), and *collaboration* between design team members requires an associated commitment to making that collaboration work.

This appreciation of design team collaboration must be recognised, at least in the context of current discussion, as representing the central line along which the course of a project can be traced. Of course, the use of shared digital models allows us to find a platform within which we can develop, store and collectively make use of project data. As an example, were I (as the quantity surveyor) to alter the specification of an insulation material within a BIM (whether it was a shared or federated model), this could potentially have implications for cost, buildability and even energy performance in the longer term. Of course, the individual who made the change could be tracked, and any clashes with other linked models would most likely be identified, but acceptance or non-challenge of the change by others in the team could arguably (and legally) constitute a collaborative and deliberate decision.

Whilst some might regard this to be an alarming situation, could we potentially take a far more positive attitude – that collaboration might become meaningful and desirable where there is an opportunity for the 'team' to contribute in a proactive manner, as opposed to being reactive to the decisions and actions of others, after the fact?

Resistance to the use of digital technologies and the importance of drawing

One objection which has been forcefully presented as an argument against the adoption of digitisation in architecture has been the importance of traditional (both manual and tactile) approaches to the development of designs, although the intrinsic connections between sketching, design and creativity continue to stimulate debate (Bilda, Gero and Purcell 2006, Belardi 2014, Scheer 2014). Such methods most obviously include the use of sketching, formal drawing and physical model making, often employed to help the designer formulate new ideas, frequently using an iterative process. One could also argue, of course, that the outputs of such methods are accessible not only to the design team, but also to the lay person, with no requirement to have access to professional expertise or to specialised equipment. One can consider in more depth, however, that this can be either facilitated or potentially hindered by the use of digital techniques. The subject of whether, and how, digital methods can be used to assist in the development of design ideas, though, is pressing. As we discussed in the preceding section, many of the early developed methods and techniques using digital drawing appear to be aimed at attempting to somehow replicate or to potentially replace manual methods of representing architecture.

One might argue that digital drafting tools, or even three-dimensional modelling software, tend to produce outputs which have quite different aesthetic qualities from those of hand drawing, but which actually serve a similar purpose in practical terms. At a very basic procedural level, the results from undertaking a two-dimensional drawing of building details using a computer are not likely to appear very different from those produced using a traditional drawing board and set square. Likewise, one could argue that outputs from many of the industry-leading three-dimensional modelling software packages produce representations of buildings which are geometrically correct and which to some extent can be modelled to show the likely effects of environmental conditions, such as daylighting and weather, on the appearance of buildings, streets and objects within the design. However, we must also recognise that this shift from manual to digital versions of what is in effect the same process does have an effect on aesthetic quality and likely perception. It might be useful to consider the ways in which the animation industry has been affected by the use of digitisation, in this respect. Although early full length animations (such as those produced by Disney in the 1930s, Lasseter 1987) were produced using entirely hand-drawn 'cells', this technique has given way over time to three-dimensional and almost photorealistic animation becoming prevalent and dominant within the industry (the work of Pixar Studios being an obvious touchpoint). Whilst I would not argue that one approach was superior to the other, surely nobody would contend that the aesthetic qualities of the approaches are identical.

Drawing as a design and communication tool

When selecting tools for any particular purpose, it is essential that the intended purpose of an activity remains foremost in the selection of methods. As proposed by Lawrence (1993) in the early 1990s, taking the position that sketching, formal technical drawing, physical model making and CAD were all available tools, one could posit that design tools (of whatever type) should all satisfy certain principles:

- account for **context specific conditions** – location, materials, environmental conditions
- **reject constraints** impinging on the design – planning, regulations, social criteria
- **encourage dialogue** and catalyse **discussion** of solutions – between designers and with stakeholders
- be able to assist in **negotiation** between diverse professional, social and aesthetic values and goals – in other words, act as a communication tool
- reflect a **long-term view**, including changing needs of users over time (and presumably environmental concerns).

(Lawrence also noted that tools could be used to critique and understand *unintended consequences* of design, presumably through simulation.)

What is interesting to note, given the time period and development of software and hardware capability in the intervening years, is that some of the concerns raised by Lawrence in the 1990s have been a focus for technical developments, whilst others have become complicated as an unintended result of that process. For example, riding the 'chasm' between viewing models and renders on a screen and the experience of being in the real world has been the focus of technical development, and the availability and accessibility of virtual and augmented reality systems have improved markedly. However, it is still far from the case that such systems are pervasive across the industry, and Lawrence's wider point about matching the communication method to the intended purpose still holds.

Lawrence also talks about the very activity of physical model making bringing value to the design process, whilst recognising that the intrinsic

Digital technologies in architectural design

Figure 2.6 Photograph of model with shallow depth of field. (Photo taken by author.)

Figure 2.7 Photograph of model with deeper depth of field affecting clarity, perception of size and communication. (Photo taken by author.)

abstraction of physical models (lacking environmental and human context) means that we must again critically assess their purpose. Certainly, in terms of assisting the designer to develop ideas in an incremental manner, as well as providing a tool for public engagement, physical models remain a powerful communication device. Considering Lawrence's suggestion that the iterative development of a model can help with the clarification and refinement of design ideas, the availability of 3D printing and rapid prototyping technology (described elsewhere in the book) has had a significant effect certainly on the speed with which physical objects can be produced, but also changed the relationship between designer and that object. Material 'printed' to produce the model is intrinsically from the digital domain, and as such may have been developed in a fundamentally different way from models produced using traditional model-making techniques. A good example of the importance of physical models in design development is contained in the description of the design process behind Woolf Architects' 'Double House' (Rattray 2003), where great emphasis is placed on returning to early material and model samples.

A well-established body of work has been reported in the literature with a specific focus on the importance of sketching within design (Van der Lugt 2005). Van der Lugt (2005) noted specifically that sketching carries three main identifiable characteristics and contributions to the design process:

- It supports a cycle of re-interpretation in the individual.
- It supports re-interpretation of the ideas of others, in a group.
- It allows and enhances access to earlier ideas.

Within other design fields, including graphic design (Schenk 1997), the use of sketching as a core part of the design process has also been recognised as being a skill which designers should value, and one which requires a place in the design curriculum. Indeed, the topic of the novice designer, as opposed to the experienced professional, and the ways in which sketching can be used to help the individual explore their own ideas, is well established. Schenk (1997) identified 25 distinct 'types' of drawing within a single study, each with a particular purpose (e.g. to note information, deal with layout, express ideas in three dimensions, demonstrate ideas, and so on), and this nuanced approach to exploring the production, value and applied purpose of drawings is vital. Indeed, it is likely to hold great value in terms of the future development of digital tools if we can understand where traditional tools, approaches and media have existing strengths. Rather than attempting to somehow replace traditional analogue methods with digital (for the sake of argument), would it not be preferable to identify where the strengths and potential of emerging digital tools might add something unique, distinctive and *useful* to the design process? That is, the introduction of digital tools might best be seen as embedding in and being complementary to existing approaches, rather than offering an 'alternative path'.

With regard to accessing earlier design ideas, it is certainly the case that many architectural projects appear to be initially driven by early sketch ideas, and that these ideas remain of critical importance as the technical design develops. Van der Lugt (2005) argues that sketching holds value in itself as a source for idea generation, and offers the possibility of a designer being able to use the sketch medium to think about design ideas as they develop, this being quite distinct from the use of sketching to 'talk' to others and convey design ideas to a wider group. The results from Van der Lugt suggested strong demonstrable connections between sketching and design ideas within the individual designer, but less strong evidence of sketches providing a strong stimuli for designers influencing each other's ideas through collaboration. This point is interesting, as it perhaps begins to suggest where efforts to study the use and development of tools to connect sketching and the digital domain can be best directed.

Another relatively recent study (Bar-Eli 2013) sheds some light on this phenomenon (the potential to use sketching to share ideas, and its limitations as a collaborative medium) by exploring the characteristics of sketches produced by a range of designers. In particular, that study explored the extent to which this can be useful in itself to inform the design process, and (in the case of that study, which used novice designers) the educational responses which might be enacted. The researchers argued that designers could be profiled as being either *learning* (recognising the solution generation process as holding educational value, perhaps related to the themes of case-based reasoning) or *designer* (with a focus on personal design and design theorisation) oriented, concluding that sketching and sketches can be used in a range of ways to support thinking and communicating and that the ways in which individual designers view and use their own sketches will vary between individuals. The value of using and also understanding sketching and its application by individuals becomes clear and opens up some questions as to how best to apply this within a collaborative setting.

Jonson (2005) was interested to explore how the use of digital technology affects the practice of sketching in design (across disciplines including architecture), and found that verbalisation and discussion of ideas appeared to be a greater driver at the very early conceptual stages, and that digital technology appeared to offer considerable potential for enhancing ideation in design (Jonson 2005). In that particular case, a range of techniques were used to capture the design experience (including self reporting, observation and interview), with Jonson identifying that verbalisation of ideas led to more 'Aha!' moments than other design methods and approaches. He noted that all participants regarded the ability to sketch as a skill, and practitioners participating in the study supported the notion that sketching be formally taught within courses.

Elsewhere in the literature (Bilda, Gero and Purcell 2006) we find some evidence to suggest that the use of sketching may not in itself influence the outcome of conceptual design in architecture, although the background of the participants in such studies appears critical. The research was also very clear to stress that there is no suggestion of conceptual designs not *existing* simply because they are not on paper – far from it, with a recognition that the concepts will exist in the mind of the designer alone (presumably making discussion of those ideas with others difficult, at least in terms of appearance if not the design intention). Bilda, Gero and Purcell (2006) appeared to show that within a single architect there was very considerable similarity between concept designs produced using a process of iterative sketching and designs emerging from think-aloud dialogue, with only the 'final' concept sketched afterwards. The researchers hypothesised that sketching might allow for recording of ideas as they develop and put less 'cognitive load' on the designer. An important point with regard to education was that students learning to design will require sketching not only to help them develop ideas, but also to better understand how ideas develop. By comparison, the expert and experienced architects involved in the study appeared able to retain the design process mentally, including associations between elements of the design, and so on. This is in agreement with much earlier work (Suwa and Tversky 1997), which explored how the design cycle, using hand-drawn sketching, consisted of a series of iterative cycles, and that the experienced designer was able to deal with longer 'chunks' of design development than the novice. The development of the interface itself also appears to be critical to the success of integrating CAD as part of the conceptual design process (Ibrahim and Pour Rahimian 2010), with evidence that CAD tools designed to support the development of technical drawings can hinder the design process if applied at earlier stages, or by novice designers.

Following such a discussion, I would tend to argue that the benefits of digitisation in terms of participation and stakeholder engagement are likely to live somewhere other than through the replication of traditional drawing and modelling tools. We could certainly now spend time exploring how architectural drawings may or may not be understandable to the layperson, and this is certainly a subject which has been studied to some extent within academia (Lawrence 1983). However, more recent advances in digitisation, including the ways in which the internet can be used to share, develop and debate information of all kinds, are arguably of more interest to the subject matter of this book. It would seem obvious that the ability to develop from and respond to the insertion of data within design models themselves is significantly different from what has come before. It is also arguable that the relatively recent technical ability to share, debate and inform models through the engagement of stakeholders and the layperson represents a significant change in how the industry can operate.

The following sections in this chapter will deal in turn with how models are now moving on from dealing simply with visual representation to becoming models which are dynamic and which can simulate all manner of influences on a design, be these environmental, social or economic. Techniques which can be used to support the communication of such models, both within the design team and to a wider audience, will then be explored.

Development of ideas through simulation

In the early 2000s, eCAADe[6] presented work which explored the key issues facing the future of CAAD within education (Mark, Martens and Oxman 2003). In that paper, one important question was whether architecture is 'building' or if architecture is regarded as 'design'. This was presented as a pedagogical problem, but can equally be regarded as a positioning question which has become key as the industry has begun to move towards information modelling. It is clearly important and meaningful to think of the design process from a philosophical perspective, in that the process itself must engage with important social, aesthetic, environmental and other concerns. Indeed, it is many of these issues which underpin and drive the examples we present of practical applications elsewhere in the book. Nevertheless, where digital models are developed in such a way that they contain technical information about components, details, materials specification and the construction process itself, the outcome of work undertaken by the 'design team' is undeniably in the realm of 'building'. There should of course be a seamless connection between the two, but the purpose and application of simulation present a challenge. What are we intending to simulate, exactly, and how might the outcomes of that simulation be assessed? Can we connect those simulated outcomes back to the aspirations of the designer at the conceptual stage, and begin to explore how the technically simulated outcomes from a technical design connect back to wider social, cultural and aesthetic values?

Information visualisation within education

One aspect of this discussion which we have not touched upon so far is that of education of the design team. As noted earlier in the work of

Eastman (1974) and others, the importance of understanding the implications of CAAD within architectural design and design processes has been recognised since the 1970s, and this has seen some parallel discussion concerning the place of computing within education pertaining to architecture and the built environment (Purcell 1980). Purcell noted that such education would often include both computing hardware and the application of suitable and relevant software, whilst also noting (in 1980) that there was a dominance of teaching relating to computer *programming*, perhaps with a desire to enable students to engage with simulation of sorts. There was also an interesting distinction made between novice and expert *users* of CAAD systems, and experts in the *development* of such systems. That is, a designer wishing to use CAAD tools might have little interest in undertaking programming themselves, but might benefit from collaboration with programmers (with regard to extending software capabilities, or suchlike).

Mark, Martens and Oxman (2003) also reported that a number of key issues had emerged through both academic research and practice which would benefit from attention. One aspect of the research at that time dealt with the prior knowledge of students (and presumably staff, across a cohort) with regard to digital skills and knowledge of its capabilities and potential. One might argue (Harrington and O'Connell 2016, Johnson, Gardner and Sweetser 2016) that the intervening years have perhaps led to a different situation, where the likelihood is no longer that students will require basic tuition in 3D modelling or even 3D 'design thinking', but that the pervasive use of digital modelling as a recreational pastime will have begun to have an effect on what the student will regard as basic tools of the trade. This perhaps connects with another point raised by Mark et al. (2003), that the practice and protocols with which students are already familiar may require tuition and guidance (although one could also argue that the shift of a professional modeller from visually to information-based models is no greater). One could also argue that the digital skills and existing abilities of students entering design education now are likely to outstrip those of existing staff, in some instances.

The connected themes of demonstrating the *potential* for the use of digital design tools in architecture and the built environment, and the need to understand and recognise how this can present both benefits and difficulties when applied in conjunction with non-digital approaches, are crucial. Oxman suggested that educators themselves need to understand whether digital architecture should be integrated as part of the mainstream or taught as a separate strand. This connects with points made by others (Coyne, Park and Wiszniewski 2002, Jonson 2005) that a focus within the development of CAAD software and hardware on production stages of architecture and building constrains the extent to which they have been applied at the conceptual and ideation stages, and the extent to which we can benefit from the intrinsic ability of new devices and approaches to catalyse new practice and theory. Likewise, design strategy should explicitly consider whether design processes are confined to traditional approaches, but in any case should explore and understand these as a core part of the *educational* design process.

Within architecture and architectural design education, teaching has traditionally taken place within a physical studio environment, although the past decade or so has seen such a rapid evolution and change with regard to multimedia and the possibilities of virtual collaboration of design teams that there now exists the opportunity to integrate such technology within the studio environment. Pektaş (2015) noted that terminology concerning the use of a *virtual design studio* emerged in the 1990s (Wojtowicz 1995) and became the focus for a study, with research concerning the use of the Internet, massive multi-user online platforms and the increasing use of virtual and augmented reality to convey architectural design. Pektaş (2015) posed a series of important research questions, against three key themes:

- the **sociocultural context** of design education – the need for designers to appreciate the connected importance of technical, social, economic and other factors, and learn to synthesise these within design
- the need for a **theoretical framework**, with regard to the virtual design studio – that is, not only to have a framework for teaching the technical approaches to virtual design, but also to foster and promote a deep understanding of how such working practice might rely on social and interpersonal skills, perhaps complemented by but certainly integrated with technical solutions
- **student opinion** and **reaction** to changes in the studio environment.

Referring to the seminal writings of (Schön 1983), Pektaş reflected on the importance of face-to-face social interaction within the studio environment, but with an informed understanding of how this might bring value to the design process. That is, where the virtual studio itself is designed in such a way that it can support interaction between designers, and encourage rather than stifle intuitive design and creativity, this may in fact open opportunities which have not been available previously. It is also interesting to read and reflect on the idea that the use of a design studio in education has a basis in both the need to develop skills within students and a need to simulate work in practice.

Pektaş (2015) then goes on to suggest that a virtual design studio should attempt to blend traditional approaches to design with new technology, whilst also benefiting from the apparent affordances of those technologies. Within such a framework, there would appear to be opportunities to augment the intelligence of the design team through:

- **blending** of traditional and online **techniques** (allowing for teams which can be partially co-located, but this not being a constraint to membership)
- **combining numerous tools**, making the importance of sharing data, ideas and outputs between tools important
- supporting the use of **cloud computing**, including provision of access to external information
- using online social media to **facilitate discussion**
- **guiding participation**.

Both the use of cloud computing and the use of guided participation and collaboration (perhaps using design protocols) have been studied elsewhere (Leon et al. 2014) and tended towards demonstrating that a process (protocol to be followed or mediated) is required to closely consider the use of technology, to ensure that it is in fact helpful in supporting the progression of design, and does not suppress the potential benefits of using technology in the first place.

Previous work (Rohrmann and Bishop 2002) has demonstrated that while computer simulations can obviously only approximate reality, they are acceptable to most people as valid representations of the real world. Other research (Heft and Nasar 2000, for example) found that although studies of environmental perception and aesthetics have traditionally been conducted using photographs or slides, reactions to static displays do not parallel those of dynamic displays. Interestingly, they found that preferences were significantly lower for dynamic compared to static conditions. This finding has implications for the way in which architectural and urban designs are presented to people – a building may look appealing in a sketch or CAAD model, but 'using' a building means that we do not experience it in static form.

Bearing this in mind, it is useful to reflect on the definition provided by Chen (2005) for the subject of information visualisation:

> as visual representations of the semantics, or meaning, of information. In contrast to scientific visualisation, information visualisation typically deals with non-numeric, nonspatial, and high-dimensional data.

This definition is useful in that it makes very clear the implication that information visualisation is different in intention and methods from approaches typically used to represent 'scientific' data. For example, data concerning the bearing capacity of a particular material will typically be numerical in nature, and might be easily represented using fairly mundane and very familiar visualisation techniques such as histograms. Whilst one might hesitate, when considering the visualisation of all data concerning the built environment, to remove the possible inclusion of such data (or data concerning cost, for example) from our discussions, we should also try to consider how non-numeric, spatial and dimensioned data, such as design concept ideas, or social impact data, might be represented in a manner which will be understood by those who need to participate in the planning, design, construction, maintenance or other processes affecting a building or area.

Aspects of the foregoing discussion tended to emphasise the potential for the use of digital technology as a part of design, and to provide an effective and useful part of the design outcome. Other studies have also identified the potential for using 3D digital models to convey ideas and concepts, engage students and lead to deeper understanding. Examples certainly abound within heritage studies (Bustillo et al. 2015), taking us

Figure 2.8 **Visualisation of greenspace using combined image and text. (Image produced by Stephen Scott.)**

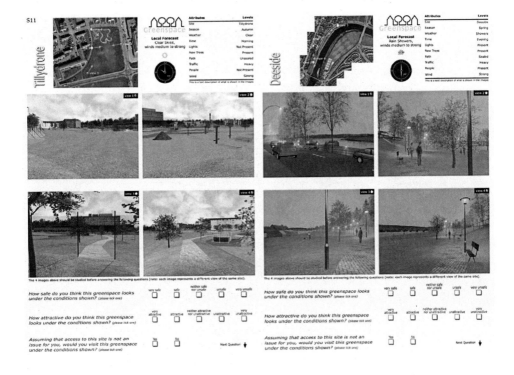

back to a consideration of digital visualisation as a communication tool. One could argue that the combined use of photogrammetry[7] and scanning most certainly holds value and potential within teaching, even when dealing with derelict or debilitated structures, and that this is likely to gain greater value still when combined with social and cultural historical study. The study presented by Bustillo and colleagues (2015) applied methods of digital virtual reconstruction, but in combination with the study of history and art with the goal of stimulating interest in both the core subject matter and the technical method being applied.

Chen's (2005) suggested challenges facing the visualisation process, nevertheless, have a broader use, and serve to focus consideration of the subject matter:

- usability
- understanding elementary perceptual–cognitive tasks
- prior knowledge
- education and training
- intrinsic quality measures
- scalability
- aesthetics
- paradigm shifts towards dynamic interpretation of data
- causality, visual inference and prediction
- knowledge domain visualisation.

Whilst not all of Chen's key issues appear to have an immediate impact on the design and use of visualisation packages in the built environment, all do in fact have implications for the manner in which we might use such packages in the future.

Usability

A commonly discussed thread of research, and the first of Chen's challenges, concerns usability. This is related to interface design, but is also deeply connected with concerns over the purpose of a software package, and the likely user of the software. Laing et al. (2007) explored many such issues, with particular reference to the use of an interactive model of a historic built environment. That study confirmed that the user's prior knowledge and expectations were vital components of how a system would be used. There were also important human–computer interface (HCI) questions which require consideration when dealing with moving images, including those of perception of scale and user comfort.

A common issue affecting many early examples of CAAD packages was that the packages themselves had an over-reliance on geometrical accuracy, which did little to foster their use at the earlier stages of the design process. Similarly, methods commonly used to present planning solutions to members of the lay-public include top-down plan views and construction details – methods of communication not typically found outside of technical circles.

Therefore, we should consider how the extent to which a package is 'usable' will vary not only between packages, but also between users and between intended tasks. Any particular CAAD system might be perfect for one task, yet entirely unsuitable for another. For example, within my own research we made extensive use of 3D Studio to produce visual representations of street and landscape environments, allowing us to generate rendered outputs. However, we would not have been able to output technical detail drawings directly from the models, or to embed elemental data. The implications of this become important as we now move towards an industry where there is potential for the domination of 'simulation software' and BIM, where multiple disciplines and individuals will be required to interact with virtual models, and with each other using IT-supported means.

Understanding elementary perception-cognition tasks

Until very recently, it has been usual for software packages used within the architecture and engineering industries to be aimed at and used by single discipline groups. Although participants will usually constitute part of a larger group, or design team, problems of interoperability between users have abounded for many years.

As multi-user object oriented packages become more popular, it is likely that numerous members of a multidisciplinary design team will find themselves sharing and working together on the same virtual model. Although such a situation has been common within engineering and the oil and gas sectors for some time, this is not the case within smaller-scale built environment projects. Consideration needs to be given to the manner in which such a potentially disparate group of skilled team members can be enabled to understand the visualised data, which might include information pertaining to materials, cost, supply chain, structure, planning and other issues. The ways in which team members interact with a model will be informed by their familiarity with the software, as well as their own discipline and pragmatic requirements. Of course, there is a further expectation that longer-term use should be made of such models, meaning that participants not involved in the original study be required to use and manipulate a model to support building maintenance.

The manner and form in which data is presented must be properly considered at the software design stage, to ensure that all members of a team 'read' the same meaning into the data presented to them. Chen's (2005) theoretical example showing a 3D dataset could easily be used to illustrate data concerning critical path analysis, or a supply chain. It is vital in such cases that the capabilities of software are used to increase clarity and to ensure that all users are clear as to the intended meaning.

Prior knowledge

In relation to visualisation in the built environment, the issue of prior knowledge takes different forms and has different implications depending on the situation or the intention of the project. To focus initially on prior knowledge of a software package, familiarity with the interface and meaning of the output is clearly essential for all core users. That is, those members of a design team who may be required to interact with the software will be required to understand the software's operation, and also the manner in which information can be retrieved, displayed, printed and otherwise exported (to other packages, for example).

This is a subtly different situation from that facing a design team exploring design issues with a client, or with affected members of the public. Issues of site topography, materials, texture, spatial layout and the experience of visiting a real place are arguably almost impossible to convey effectively to the layperson using traditional 2D plans and elevations. In such a situation, prior knowledge of a site on the part of the client would enhance the communication process, if only to provide a context in terms of the existing site and surroundings. In such cases, it may well be the case that detail showing the position and relative size of existing landmarks (e.g. prominent nearby buildings, major roads, open spaces, etc.) may in fact be as important as providing detailed information on a new development. That is, prior knowledge in such cases may demand that consideration of the *impact* of a design on a known environment will be vital.

Aesthetics

With many built environment projects, it is very much the case that the site and project will be difficult (aesthetically) to represent in total photo realism, due to the complex nature of built and constructed spaces. Quite apart from the dynamic nature of built spaces (see Chen's 2005 plea for 'dynamic representation', for example), where movement of participants and traffic is central to the experience of a place, it is also true that aesthetic preferences are driven as much by constituent parts of a scene (Laing et al. 2006), as they may be by an overall impression of 'beauty'.

These issues may prove useful when considering the practical value and applicability of various techniques, methods and theories. However, one should also remember that Chen himself suggests that the list is certainly not comprehensive, and that other issues and fields might be or become equally important in the future.

The purpose of any form of visualisation or modelling will often be to elucidate information or a problem. Particularly within architecture and other built environment disciplines, models will be used for a range of tasks from the design stage through to life cycle management. These stages may be related in terms of the facility or building, but might require quite different approaches to modelling and to data storage. Rather than concentrate immediately on each stage of the 'process', it might be more useful to instead consider the range of purposes to which models may be put.

Firstly, and most obviously, models of buildings can be used to represent the likely final appearance of that building. Abstract models lacking 'detail' of the final materials tend to be commonly used at the conceptual stages of the design process. Such models are useful as they provide the design team with a common object through which ideas can be discussed, developed and debated. Although some studies have shown that 2D, 3D and moving representations tend to be perceived by experts and non-experts differently, there is also a strong argument that such 'abstract' models can be used to discuss design solutions with a client at the outset, thus framing what may be the large issues (e.g. spatial layout, overall structure and form) without becoming distracted by details of where each part of the budget may reside. One could also argue that the financial impact of a design may in fact be deeply wedded to the structure and overall form of a building design, and that even abstract models can be utilised to illustrate where aspects (such as service location or room layout) could be altered to drive the design towards a more efficient solution.

This in some ways brings us back to consider the subject of 2D as opposed to 3D representations of space. Although much of the emphasis now placed on the development of new computer modelling systems is focused on the use of 3D methods, it is certainly true that many examples of historical cutting edge information visualisation involved two-dimensional representations of space or concepts.

Digital technologies in architectural design

Figure 2.9
Elevation view from laser scan data. (Image produced by Dr Marianthi Leon.)

Figure 2.10
Perspective view from laser scan data. (Image produced by Dr Marianthi Leon.)

Where modelling has more recently been undertaken in three dimensions, using IT-based systems, the practical benefits beyond those associated with the purely aesthetic consideration of a space have become apparent. Although this can in some ways relate to the topic of prototyping and virtual testing, the increasing availability of systems based around object-oriented modelling has allowed designers to produce models which capture not only the appearance but also the physical characteristics of a structure.

A further development in recent years, which certainly relates also to the growth of GIS (geographical information system) within planning and design, is that of nD modelling. By this, we refer to models where the data contained within extends beyond geometrical data to include, for example, scheduling, costing, accessibility, crime, sustainability, maintainability, acoustics and energy simulation (Aouad, Lee and Wu 2005).

Where the model produced to assist with the design and construction of a building is sufficiently detailed to capture all aspects of the building, there is a strong argument that the model should be regarded as a valuable asset to be drawn on during the life cycle. This is particularly true of any model which purports to contain information regarding materials and their performance. Such data is clearly useful at the design stage to support analysis of the initial construction cost, but could equally be used to drive an analysis of life cycle concerns that include maintenance, replacement and energy costs.

Theories of information visualisation have developed over the past 20 years, and that development has taken place both at the theoretical cross-discipline level and also within disciplines at the level of application and understanding. Before we become overly concerned with the extent to which computers and IT can influence the way in which we develop ideas of visualisation within current built environment projects, it is worthwhile to take a step back and consider how 'visualisation' can be and has been used to successfully present information and data in a manner which is illuminating and immediate to the user. An appreciation of such approaches then allows us to see how successful design of the often IT dependent approaches taken nowadays in the built environment relies on a more basic understanding of visual communication to ensure success.

Summary

In this chapter we have begun to draw together a number of different strands of discussion. Importantly within these were themes central to information visualisation, where we could trace seminal examples of the use of visualisation and visual communication to convey complex ideas and situations in a manner which was widely accessible. These themes and different practices are important, as they serve to show us how the choice of communication method can have a significant effect on the insights which can be drawn from the underlying information. Thinking for a moment about our earlier discussions of drawing and sketching, we are again reminded of studies which have demonstrated important truths about the use of visual communication to help both individuals and teams to develop their ideas, and to do so in a collaborative manner.

We also began to think in more depth about the notions of collaboration, and how these might be supported by or even stimulated by the use of digital technology. Within the consideration of BIM, it was interesting to note how some models of the maturity of use were almost defined by the extent to which participants in the design process were engaged and taking part in active collaboration.

Later chapters deal with various examples of emerging technology and consider how these might be brought to bear to help support collaboration within teams, as well as enhanced levels of user participation in design. It is important that we bear in mind these principles of communication and collaboration as we now move on to consider how they may be applied within practice.

Notes

1. An open access version is available for viewing via https://upload.wikimedia.org/wikipedia/commons/2/29/Minard.png (accessed 18 April 2018).
2. Further biographical and other information on Minard can be found via this link: www.edwardtufte.com/tufte/minard-obit (accessed 18 April 2018).
3. A wider discussion of what is, and is not, meant by BIM can be found at www.bimtaskgroup.org/bim-faqs/ (accessed 18 April 2018).
4. www.cpic.org.uk (accessed 18 April 2018).
5. Construction (Design and Management) Regulations 2015 were introduced by the Health and Safety Executive. Also known as the CDM Regulations, they are legally binding and aim to improve health and safety within the industry.
6. eCAADe (Education and research in Computer Aided Architectural Design in Europe) is a non-profit making association of institutions and individuals, founded in 1983, with a common interest in promoting good practice and sharing information in relation to the use of computers in research and education in architecture and related professions. Further information is available via http://ecaade.org (accessed 18 April 2018).
7. Where photogrammetry provides the means to create 3D surface models and extract relative proportions from photographs of an object, as opposed to on-site measurement, scanning or the like.

Chapter 3

Digital visualisation in practice

This chapter explores the prevalent use of visualisation to foster collaborative working within design teams, ideas generation, use of visualisation in marketing of architecture and in the operation of buildings. The chapter also draws on specific examples from industry to illustrate the emerging themes, and in particular gives practical indications of how technology can be applied in practice to promote and foster collaboration and team working.

One needs to be aware of the balance to be struck between the further development of existing technologies (iterations) and the possibility of completely new approaches and ideas taking the industry and practice in unexpected directions. This was at the core of arguments developed by Scheer (2014), which drew attention to the fact that whilst building information modelling *appears* to produce design outputs similar to those of software designed to replicate the drawing board, the *actual* outputs are in fact very different. Likewise, whilst virtual collaboration (distant working, digital sharing of models, the virtual studio) might appear at first glance to simply replicate traditional approaches and organisation of the design office, the implications for communication, understanding what is *actually* being shared and the nature of the final output (including authorship) are profound.

Collaborative working – the digital studio
This and the following section start to deal in more detail with the technical reality of collaborative working, how this can be assisted by digitisation, and where visualisation of information can be used to assist with that process. They have been deliberately separated to reflect the fact that collaborative working will operate in a different manner if people are actually co-located (by which I mean, located in same room or

in the same office), as opposed to if people are working across great distances.

Where people are in the same location as each other, we must again refer back to earlier discussions about the appropriate use of technology, and attempting to ensure that any digital processors or tools are selected and then applied so that they best match the problem to hand. Therefore, in the case where people are working out of the same office, an emphasis on methods to help with distant person-to-person communication (for example, the use of videoconferencing) is likely to be far less relevant to the team than the application of techniques which augment the existing studio setting. This section, though, will also deal with and consider a situation where people may be simultaneously working for the same organisation, and may in fact be part of an extended yet temporary design team, but where there is actually a need to have some form of virtual studio. This may also refer to instances where members of the team are actually working away from the office, or are temporarily located on-site, or where there is an important reason to communicate with external parties.

The idea of the virtual studio is one which has appeared regularly within academic publications, and has become increasingly important within the industry itself. Indeed, although this is not a book limited to the discussion of BIM, some of the aspirations connected with higher-level adoption of building information modelling are almost defined by the idea that the design team may in fact be located in disparate positions, yet still working as a fully collaborative and fully integrated team. It is interesting at this stage to consider some previous studies, and some previous and current examples from industry, to gain a deep understanding of the virtual studio. The following sections deal with both the social and technical challenges of working in any virtual environment, but also start to identify and critically discuss opportunities which have arisen in recent years, responding to long-held aspirations which have only lately become practically possible. Work from the early 1990s (Mitchell 1994) concerning the development of computer-aided design touched upon the notion of this being intrinsically connected with collaboration in design, albeit pre-dating a pervasive use of the Internet in anything like the form which we know today. Mitchell characterised three paradigms to help us understand or at least conceptualise how computer-aided design could usefully develop in the future:

- designing as problem solving
- designing as a knowledge-based activity
- designing as a social activity.

With particular reference to collaborative working, it is useful to consider the third of these paradigms, where Mitchell gives consideration to the kinds of digital tools which might be required to support open discussion among a multidisciplinary design team. He appears to describe various versions of a digital modelling process which mirror some aspects of BIM maturity definitions, for example locally stored versions of the model, versions which are jointly owned and edited, connected with some kind of technology which facilitates discussion and debate. Where Mitchell extends the discussion into what he terms the use of artificial intelligence in design, we can perhaps begin to recognise aspects of computer-aided simulation which are now reasonably common within the industry. One could argue that the virtual studio should be characterised as a 'social technical system', where technology is applied to help ensure that intelligence and information can be shared and distributed (Pektaş 2015).

Collaborative working – online and distant communication

The preceding section raised some interesting points regarding the drivers, as well as the digital tools and techniques, which can be applied to support the establishment of a virtual studio. Within the industry itself, there is a long-held tradition stretching back many hundreds of years regarding the studio and the étalier, within which design work would be undertaken, debated and finalised. In our earlier discussion of the importance of drawing, we argued that digital techniques are probably best developed and designed to do something other than simply replace analogue techniques. In the case of sketching and hand drawing, for example, our earlier review established the ways in which simple tools (a pencil and a piece of paper) are probably ideally suited to certain types of creativity, ideas iteration and even sharing of ideas between designers. However, this does not mean that complementing these by using digitisation is in any way indicative of having taken a wrong turn. I would argue quite the opposite, although there is a danger that the incredible depth of value and richness of ideas which are inherent within the hand-drawing process become lost as we find ourselves participating in a march towards information-rich models of the built environment.

This section, then, deals with ways in which collaborative working can be supported using digitisation and digital techniques, and can expand beyond participants who are located within some form of design team. One of the notable characteristics of the development of digital architecture has been the wide and varied range of contexts within which the technology has begun to be applied. This has certainly included the development of new digital technologies, and in particular software and model viewers, which can be used by various members of a wide design team to interact with digital information. This helps to counteract some perhaps early concerns about the technical ability of each design team member to interact with digital models. The reality has been, and is likely to continue to be, that models can be used to support the discipline specific tasks and duties of each design team member, with those tasks and duties not necessarily varying considerably from what was undertaken traditionally.

Considering one role within the design team, that of the quantity surveyor, it is fascinating to view a process taking place within the context of quantification, measurement and costing which is not unlike the development we have seen within both architecture and engineering in terms of new and innovative digital tools. For example, the tools available to the architect have long since extended beyond simple methods through which people can sketch on a computer, instead of sketching on a piece of paper. Software advances have meant that whilst it is certainly possible for practitioners to limit their digital experience to replication and replacement of analogue tools with digital alternatives, a much more obvious path to follow has been to utilise digital tools which allow a far wider range of possibilities (environmental analysis, 'live' and informed comparison with models produced by other members of the team, integration with other sources of data such as material collected through laser scanning). Similarly, early iterations of computer software aimed at the quantity surveyor tended to be based around replicating tasks which had previously been undertaken through a process of manual measurement, with handwritten draft material then being passed to secretarial support staff to convert into formalised legal documents. This software development process has now been transformed, in that it is possible to extract quantities from the 3D models themselves, and much of the software which has been developed then makes it possible to directly connect these processes with cost analysis and with much later stages of the construction and even beyond into the working life cycle.

It is interesting to consider how digital tools can enable collaboration – not just within the design team, as was described in the previous section, but also where members of the design team are actually located in quite different positions. In larger construction projects this is likely to be the normal situation in many instances, but the possibility to much more fully integrate practitioners who simply cannot visit the site in person, but whose expertise would be hugely beneficial to the project, has become far easier in recent years.

The other major topic which we will deal with in this section is that of participatory design and engagement in community planning processes.

In Chapter 5 we explore specific examples of research, within which I have been involved personally, which attempted to use digital visualisation and online engagement tools to explore the ways in which members of the wider community, and certainly members of the community outside of the design and decision-making teams, could participate more fully in design matters. These included local residents and community groups, and concerned design of streets, access to greenspace and attitudes towards the built heritage.

Design research has identified the challenges and opportunities of attempting to work across distributed (often virtual) teams and locations, whilst recognising that the importance of sketching within a studio setting cannot simply be allowed to disappear or be ignored due to participants being distant from one another. One study (Eris, Martelaro and Badke-Schaub 2014) compared the experience, process and outputs from comparable design processes where one group was operating using digital tools to support shared sketch ideas, whilst the other was co-located. The importance of gesturing and speech (dialogue between design team members) was found to be critical. Again we can consider our earlier discussion of the medium through which people might communicate. Whilst the distributed (virtual) team used a system of vertical digital screens and cameras to communicate, the co-located team used whiteboards, presumably to mirror the ICT of the other group as much as to replicate a normal design environment. One can imagine that a design team in practice might be inclined to make use of a range of traditional analogue tools (paper, physical model making, tracing paper) as well as digital tools. Indeed, this multi-faceted approach to design technology perhaps represents the most likely one to be taken in practice, albeit one which is difficult to study in such a controlled environment.

With reference to valuable theoretical models of the design process and the participants involved (Demirkan 2005), one can begin to appreciate that collaboration might be understood to exist and be vital at all stages of design and delivery:

- users: designers, engineers, technicians
- information 'agents': legislation, codes, expert domains.

Where collaboration might take place over the web, and using digital communication, though, the importance of 'communication agents' to mediate between users and facilitate discussion is key. Evidence would tend to suggest that the quality of an overall project will increase in line with the quality of communication between users, and that communication using sketching can be facilitated over the Internet.

Ideas generation through collaboration

One key theme in this book, and one which has formed a very significant strand of research within architecture over the past 40 to 50 years, has been that of participating in design. In the case of some research, this has mainly taken the form of studies and examples from practice which try to engage with end users in a variety of interesting and creative ways. We touch on many of these studies elsewhere in the book, and begin to understand how a range of methods (both analogue and digital) can be used by a designer and by a design team to try to better involve people, communities and groups who might be affected by the outcomes of the design, once fabricated or constructed. Of course, it should also be noted that the theories and practice of participatory architectural design have been studied for many years, with clear lines of development since the 1960s (as noted and described by Sanoff 2011).

What we are more concerned about is the specific subject of collaboration. This is arguably quite distinct from approaches where we can use methods and technology when attempting to enhance or stimulate processes of consultation or even deeper participation in design. It is nevertheless prudent that we consider how technology has been useful in helping the designer to generate ideas, working in the role of an independent designer. Research which studied the effect of technology in such circumstances provides us with some useful insights regarding the ways in which technology can support ideas proposed by a designer, but where the technology might in itself begin to shape those ideas. Whether the shaping of design ideas by the technology itself (and by technology, in this context, I refer to both software and hardware) can be useful, or even desirable, is certainly open for debate, and will be discussed towards the end of the section.

One very significant danger which I would argue faces the construction industry as a whole is the fact that whilst digital technology certainly does exist which is capable of supporting collaborative working (for example, through the use of shared digital models, or technology which allows team members to work at a distance from one another), this does not mean that either collaboration within the industry or indeed working practices which embrace the participation of end users are any more likely to automatically find a place within practice than they have in the past. This is analogous, in terms of the challenge which lies ahead, to the clichéd problem of taking a horse to water in the hope that it will drink. In the case of collaborative working, we as an industry must recognise that collaboration and working in a collaborative manner require the development of new skills, and that collaborative practice is an activity which requires just that – practice.

Similarly, an important thread running through the text of this book concerns the ways in which digital technology and visualisation tools can be used to help support the participation of end users, as part of the design process. In this context, it is necessary for us to recognise that whilst there may be a need for participation, and this could possibly be imposed on a design team (maybe by the client or even through legislation in certain circumstances), the ways in which this might actually happen would always run the risk of paying insufficient heed to well-established models of best practice. That is to say, just because models appeared to suggest ways that individuals or groups can exchange information, this does not mean that the resulting communication is going to be insightful, meaningful or even useful to the participants. Therefore, the development of digital tools to support participation in design needs to go hand-in-hand with a realisation of that best practice, but also a recognition that both education and applied practice will form a necessary part of the learning curve.

This perspective is very useful when attempting to understand how technology might begin to support, and even affect, the processes and outcomes of collaborative design. By 'collaborators' in this sense we refer to the notion that a collective design team is working as a 'team', throughout the design process. Again referring back to our earlier discussions of the aims of the industry, stretching back certainly to the 1990s and probably earlier, and forming a major driver for the implementation of the likes of BIM, a desire to develop the design and construction team which is focused on collaboration, as opposed to the combat of working relationships, has been long held. I would argue, at this stage, that technology can certainly only be part of the solution to this particular problem. As others have studied and written, some of the issues which require addressing in order to move towards a more collaborative working environment within the architecture and construction industries reside at an organisational level within management structures, and at the personal level demand that we understand psychological and even sociological cause and effect.

Now, we are perhaps better equipped to appreciate and understand the ways in which technology can build support for and influence the work of the designer. We are also well equipped to understand what the aspirations of an industry with deeper levels of collaboration might actually be, in terms of the desired end goal. What I would argue at this stage is that simply providing technology which supports the easy sharing of files and the data contained within those files is not in itself likely to produce a transformed industry. After all, it was always possible for an architect to provide the quantity surveyor and the engineer with drawings. Likewise, it was always possible for the quantity surveyor to provide other members of the team with information pertaining to costings, quantification and suchlike. If we seriously aspire to use technology to encourage deep and meaningful collaboration between members of the design team, and between multiple disciplines, then we need to ensure that software and also the models of data management, storage and use are likewise geared towards supporting collaboration.

Summary

Within this chapter we gave some deeper consideration to the application of emerging digital technology to support work within design teams, including the notion of the virtual design studio, and technology which could be used to support virtual and distributed working. Aspects of the subject matter can be regarded as central to the manner in which the industry is likely to develop in the coming years. This will include the sharing of digital artefacts and other such data, but also the reality of team members being required to engage fully in collaborative practice, but having to do so whilst working at a distance from their closest colleagues.

As argued in previous chapters, it is important that we do not mistake the availability of technology (which in the case of this chapter dealt with distant communication) with a corresponding commitment on the part of design team participants to work to overcome the inherent limitations of such technology, whilst also managing the potential benefits, which may in fact be unique to the technology itself.

Finally, we then also considered the ways and extent to which collaboration between team members can in itself be regarded as an ideas generation process. This is certainly worth bearing in mind as we begin to look at the democratic use of visualisation. Some may argue that there exists the potential when undertaking design processes or research studies with a wide constituency of respondents for that constituency to lead to uninspiring (lowest common denominator) design solutions, but by fully considering and planning for the use of collaboration in practice one could also argue that the potential for inspiration might be realised.

Chapter 4

Democratic visualisation

As digital visualisation has become more advanced in terms of hardware and software capabilities (e.g. building information modelling, digital infrastructure, HD laser scanning), there has been a corresponding development of methods which are inexpensive and accessible (e.g. photogrammetry). The impact of this democratisation of the economics and accessibility of visualisation, where anybody can take part, will be explored. Examples from urban study and the built heritage are included by way of illustration.

Many of the techniques and technologies described in earlier chapters might be regarded as being out of the reach of a large number of potential participants in architectural design. Among these we could include the use of advanced visualisation techniques and tools, where augmented and virtual reality have, until recently, required advanced skills which are outside of the 'normal' construction industry. There is also the issue of cost, in that the price of hardware (e.g. laser scanning) when coupled with a need for post-processing of data represents a considerable financial outlay. This is an important consideration, as there is a need for a widespread ability to view, interact with and potentially alter or add to computer-based models. It is also an important consideration regardless of whether we are dealing with what might be termed the professional design team, or we are considering the contribution of a much wider constituency (such as occupants of a town or city, who may wish to influence or contribute to digital models and modelling).

Several 3D data collection techniques have emerged recently, including scanning, photogrammetry, virtual modelling, 3D printing and rapid prototyping to capture information about existing buildings and environments. Together, these support BIM-enabled design decision making. The primary strength of object oriented BIM models is that they are able to incorporate detailed and layered information pertaining to the environment represented. However, a practical challenge facing the design team working either with an existing building or within a site context which affects existing buildings is that of how to include accurate data reflecting the pre-existing environment.

In the previous chapter, we discussed the desirability of the wider design team being able to collaborate using digital tools. In some cases, this might well involve numerous participants and organisations being able to undertake detailed modelling work, and thus requiring the necessary hardware and software, as well as digital modelling skills, to allow this to happen. However, other members of the design team may not actually need to have access to such capabilities, for example where their main requirement might be to simply view models to extract information (quantities, specification, construction details). This is where the ability of information-rich models to be shared using open source file formats comes into its own.

The other main context which requires discussion and attention is that of public engagement in architecture, and the extent to which digital tools can be used to support that engagement in a meaningful manner. This has in itself been a major area of research for many years within the disciplines which one would recognise as falling within the design team; it is also a subject which has received attention within psychology, planning and environmental design.

Methods

Methods which can be usefully employed within the construction industry to record the existing built environment have included fairly traditional hands-on approaches, such as physical measurement, sketching, photography as well as traditional site levelling and surveying. Over the course of the last decade, though, these approaches have been supplemented by the emergence of advanced digital measurement tools, such as laser scanning. One thing which has certainly made these techniques less applicable to the non-expert user has, ironically, not been the necessary skills base (as the techniques have become incrementally more straightforward), but rather the financial cost of adoption.

High definition scanners operate by firing laser light to collect many millions of data points, which together offer a representation of the space surrounding the scanner head as a 'cloud' of dots. The time required to undertake a single scan varies but can be as little as 1 to 2 minutes to collect a high definition cloud. Again depending on the equipment, a single scan can cover ranges of up to approximately 200 metres, and the resultant point cloud can be viewed from any angle and is not limited to the original position of the scanner head. With most scanners, information can be collected to represent a 'dome' around the scanner, but this is limited to collecting information about surfaces or static objects in the scan vicinity. Larger areas can be surveyed through the collection of data from multiple scanning positions, which can then be connected (registered) to form a more comprehensive representation of an area. Thus, the value of scanning within the context of urban design begins to become clearer, in that existing buildings and town layouts can be collected rapidly and potentially viewed from both human scale and strategic (top-down) angles. Similarly, and from the perspective of the architectural designer, it is possible to collect highly accurate data regarding the actual surface of buildings, such as decorative features.

With the emergence of financially accessible methods, many of which draw on photography as the main means of data collection, much wider participation in the surveying, recording and modelling of existing buildings and landscapes has become possible. That is, a participant no longer requires access to expensive equipment in order to collect data and produce perfectly usable 3D models of objects and spaces.

From the perspective of tracing widespread interest in the existing built environment, the development of a largely online movement interested in abandoned architecture (often 20th century, where buildings have fallen into disrepair through loss of the practical purpose) has been both rapid and highly participative. Whilst some of the sites arguably hold personal emotional resonance for the viewer (from my own perspective, photographs of the abandoned 'Santaland' in Aviemore are particularly emotive!), the promise of unexpected or chance encounters appears to carry mystique for many. Some recent studies and publications have reflected a widespread interest in the study and recording of 'abandoned architecture', with the accompanying text often referring as much to the social history embodied in the buildings and remnants as to the architecture itself (Leslie 2017).

In terms of methods and digital techniques, two approaches which are worth considering are those of 'tilt shift' photography and photogrammetry. My own first interaction with architectural shift lenses (I speak more of this in Chapter 5) came about when photographing building facades. However, the technical method has a peculiar side-effect on the images themselves, in that the edges tend to blur as a result of 'perspective correction'. In recent years, the term 'tilt shift effect' has tended to be applied to images where the edges (often the top and bottom of photographs) have been artificially blurred, to give the impression of there being a narrow depth of field. This would normally happen (when using a regular camera) only when photographing smaller objects, so can

Figure 4.1
Example of 'tilt shift' photographic effect. (Photo taken by author.)

Figure 4.2
Example of output from photogrammetric 3D model. (Image created by author.)

have the effect of tricking the eye into believing that we are looking at a model of an area or object, as opposed to a photograph of a street, city or landscape (Held et al. 2010).

These methods are interesting and pertinent to the themes of this book as they deal with the subject of how members of a much wider constituency than the traditional and professional design team can engage with the design process. The technologies which underpin these methods are economically and to some extent philosophically accessible to anybody who might wish to participate.

One aspect of the growth of accessible technology, with regard to both creative photography of architecture and also engagement in the processes of 3D digital modelling, which it is important for us to consider is that of the motivations which might have driven participation in the first place. In the case of tilt shift photography, for example, it would seem very doubtful that most people participating in the manipulation of digital images to produce imitated examples of tilt shift photographs are doing so as a result of some desire to experiment with the notion of photography. Indeed, it seems more likely that the ability of the method to allow the user and the participant to experiment in a very playful manner with ideas of the real in the model and somewhere in between has become a driver in itself.

Photogrammetry refers to a process whereby three-dimensional digital models are constructed using photographic images of an existing object or structure, to determine what are actually reasonable proportional representations. Although it is not directly possible from the method itself to establish accurate size data (in the manner which would be common and readily accessible using laser scanning, for example), one can argue that the main benefit of applying photogrammetry comes in terms of both cost and accessibility of the method and the hardware required. A number of studies have reported on how the method can be used to construct digital models where it was not possible to access the site using laser scanning or other such equipment, or even using a collection of photographic materials which were originally collected for quite different purposes. Some examples of the method being applied in practice provide powerful social and cultural evidence of how the approach can be used by communities wishing to document their own built environment, and also with environments which have been irrevocably damaged, altered or even destroyed by natural hazards or warfare (Themistocleous 2017). Other authors who have considered the use of photogrammetry (particularly within the context of built heritage measurement and recording) have noted that the method, perhaps working in parallel with more traditional methods of surveying (including the proportional extraction of dimensions from single photographs or even on-site surveying), provides valuable, reliable and easily compiled digital information at a range of levels, up to and including entire buildings (Yastikli 2007).

Recent work (Valero et al. 2017) noted that photogrammetry had been shown to yield effective results in comparison to hand-drawn surveys, and that the method can in fact be quite effectively combined with terrestrial laser scanning to provide more complete models of the built heritage. This is a useful insight in itself, as anybody familiar with the practice of undertaking terrestrial laser scanning will be acutely aware that whilst the method allows for the highly detailed recording of geometrical information, even where it is not possible to locate oneself in the proximity of an object, the scanner can only record what is within sight of the scanner location. This means that many surfaces of a building or streetscape might be 'blind' to the scanner (such as rooftops, inaccessible elevations, and suchlike). Valero et al. (2017) note that photogrammetry is a well-established technique within heritage modelling and recording, but that its application (including in combination with terrestrial laser scanning) should be planned with care to ensure optimal results. These considerations are of great importance, of course, particularly where the purpose of the reality capture is part of detailed design work. As with all of the other methods considered, though, this must also be matched to the intended outcomes and values of any particular study or activity. For example, if the main intention behind an exercise using photogrammetry is actually one of user engagement, or to form part of a process to actively encourage user participation in community-led design, one could argue that engagement in the collection of data as a process and as an experience might actually be valuable as an outcome in itself.

Further to this discussion, Yastikli (2007) provided an overview of digital photogrammetry and laser scanning, while also introducing the terminology 'stereo photogrammetry'. This is applied in a similar manner to traditional photogrammetry, but often using hundreds of captured photographic images, offering the possibility of a route through which photogrammetry could be used to capture information about increasingly complex architectural services and features. Software available for use with mobile technologies, utilising the cloud for calculation and formation of a 3D surface model (Autodesk Recap Photo), supports digitisation of an object, automatic detection of coordinates in photographic images (with little expertise required) and, ultimately, the rapid development of to-scale models (for digital presentation or physical 3D printing). Although geared towards the establishment of models which support surface modelling, the technique has some commonality with approaches for the collection of overall site or environment measurements, including indoor or contained environments. Freely available cloud-based software supports the export of such data as modifiable 3D surface models, which can be incorporated in typically used architectural packages such as 3DS Max and in turn most BIM packages. Reference can be made to Figure 1.3 in Chapter 1, which shows an example of a photogrammetric model taken from a church detail in Copenhagen.

Others have noted that the outputs of photogrammetry tend to be easier to interpret than the sole use of two-dimensional drawings, and that the availability of three-dimensional representations of a building or structure makes the use of such data within reconstruction or redesign projects much easier. What has become clear in some work (Núñez

Andrés et al. 2012) is that the combined use of numerous methods is likely to bring greatest benefit to the user.

One particularly interesting and prescient example from the literature describes the use of close range photogrammetry to record examples of the built heritage found along the Silk Road ancient trade route (Yilmaz, Yakar and Yildiz 2008). The study is interesting in that it considers the practicalities and efficiencies of using photogrammetry, comparing it not with other highly technology-dependent approaches but instead with the traditional approaches of attempting to take a record of the built environment using hand drawings and sketching. The researchers in that particular case found that the use of photography and photogrammetry enabled them to develop a useful and persuasive digital model in a reasonably short period of time. One can also imagine in most instances that meta data (context, materials, textures, side notes) associated with the model will certainly be as important as the geometry of the model itself.

Likewise, the widespread availability of software which supports the creation of 3D digital models from photographs has certainly been encouraged by the distribution of such software either through mobile applications or bundled with consumer-level drones. As described by Valero et al. (2017), this becomes an important consideration for both professional practice and user engagement studies, as the democratic angle here extends into both the necessary skills base and the financial outlay which is going to be required to enable participation in the first place.

One could argue, though, that the intention in both cases would have been to further drive sales of hardware (in this case mobile devices, digital cameras or drones equipped with cameras). Although some of the papers to which we refer in earlier parts of this chapter certainly debate the geometrical accuracy of some of the photogrammetric outcomes, thus bringing into question their usefulness within the industry itself, what if one were to argue that at the heart of this notion of usefulness is that of engagement of the wider community? If this technology has encouraged wide ranging engagement by a large number of individuals, who participate in the social study, cataloguing and even online debate and discussion of architecture, could one argue that this is in fact a form of engagement in architecture, if not necessarily part of a planned collaborative process?

Democratic access to technology

Notwithstanding the rapid and arguably radical reduction in the price of hardware which makes engagement with digital modelling possible, the extent to which potential users and stakeholders of such digital models have engaged with the processes has been remarkable. Regarding industry engagement, one aspect of digitisation which cannot be overstated in terms of importance is that of open access. Although with respect to BIM itself there are still obvious, clear and important arguments for data security (and these will persist), there is a corresponding need for all necessary participants in the digitisation process to be able to access, view and, where appropriate, even edit each other's models.

This is quite a significant departure from the practice of the past, where each member of the design team, where they were using digital models at all, might have had little reason to consider whether the wider team would be able to access that data. However, the development and encouragement of methods of working to assist with collaborative decision making mean that models must, at the very least, be viewable by all who are required to extract data. However, it is unlikely that all members of the team will need to, or be inclined to, actually change the model itself in terms of geometry or layout (in the case of a building), supply chain or similar information, and this will need to be undertaken by the 'design team' in its widest sense. For members of the construction team, an ability to view, interact with and extract dataflow models will be crucial, and relying on printed drawings which have been extracted and published by others is both inefficient and potentially adds confusion and inaccuracy. We will return to some technical solutions which can be enacted to assist with these processes later in the chapter.

The subject of democratic access to technology also comes to the fore when we consider the ways in which public consultation in planning and design has been affected by digitisation in recent years. This extends beyond our consideration of how people might be able to access shared models within the design team, and naturally draws us towards a consideration of viewing and interacting with models over the Internet. There are now plentiful examples of cities where models of a range of types (in terms of realism, content and interactivity) have been used to help local authorities engage with members of the public and with local communities. These methods are perhaps defined, though, to some extent by the fact that the models themselves (i.e. the structure, presentation and geometry), are by and large constructed by experts, relying on expert knowledge and information which is available to professional groups. This chapter draws attention to and discusses some key studies which have been undertaken to explore ways in which members of the public can engage using digitisation and visualisation. In recent times, though, these are typically examples of buildings and structures which came into being many years before digitisation of any kind, let alone architectural, was common or even possible. Relating back in some ways to our discussions elsewhere in the book about abandoned buildings and abandoned architecture, there has been an exponential growth in user-constructed digital models of aspects of the built heritage. Until recently, many of these models were constructed using various photogrammetry techniques, but this is likely to extend to the widespread use of laser scanning and photogrammetry using drones in the coming years. The reasons for these techniques becoming popular, both among those producing the models and those viewing and commenting on results, are fascinating and arguably have as much to do with culture and society as with technology and digitisation.

The application of technology in a democratic manner can, of course, refer to access to the technology for all, as well as the use of the technology to actually serve democratic purposes. This again prompts us to refer to the ladder of citizen participation (Arnstein 1969), and perhaps begin to query the ways in which decision making in relation to our constructed environment can be used to move from positions of top-down control towards notions of citizen control, or at the very least situations where citizens are able to make a significant and meaningful contribution to the debate. With specific reference to planning of the built environment, it has been interesting to follow the ways in which technology which has emerged from both architecture and geography has begun to have a significant influence on the way we plan and even manage our cities.

As with the ladder proposed by Arnstein, such visually driven technology can certainly be used in the service of public consultation, or simply to present and then subsequently study the likely aesthetic impact of new architecture on existing townscapes. Prominent examples from across the United Kingdom of this being applied in practice can be seen in Newcastle and Glasgow, where the respective municipal authorities have worked with local universities and partners in design practice to develop digital versions of parts of the city centre areas, including buildings and topography. In the case of Newcastle, and working closely with Northumbria University, the model also made early use of semi-immersive technology, where it was perhaps possible to better represent not only what buildings may look like in terms of still images extracted from the model, but also in terms of the experience of being in a space.

The development of a model to deal with planning and architectural design in Glasgow was undertaken by the Digital Design Studio (Glasgow School of Art), who, as an aside, were also early pioneers in the use of parametric modelling, particularly in the context of digital design of products. One element which is especially interesting about both the Glasgow and Newcastle models is that each made some effort to ensure that prominent examples of architecture within each of the cities were modelled to a higher level of detail. Each of the models was also virtually constructed using workflows and processes which would be familiar within regular architectural design. That is, we eventually arrived at versions of Newcastle and Glasgow using digital technology which allowed us to take a human eye view of cities, and where the buildings appeared (at least in early versions of models) to have been generated using various methods of block modelling.[1] This is arguably quite different from the processes which may be followed nowadays, with the widespread availability of both laser scanning and photogrammetry.

In the case of some recent work undertaken within Aberdeen, for example, the modelling work undertaken within the city centre utilised high-definition laser scans of both buildings and streetscapes, which was in turn quite different from design protocols followed by the research team to which I belonged in the mid-2000s. Using this process, through which we actually arrived at virtual versions of Aberdeen reasonably quickly, it was possible within hours of undertaking scanning work to then produce visually impressive still images from emerging models, as well as walk-throughs of the city. Furthermore, as it is now possible to both open and interact with scan data in the regular industry-standard modelling packages (such as REVIT), a perceived need to immediately proceed towards block modelling, where scan data was used as a basis for such modelling, became diminished. That is, just as one could argue that an architectural block model is nothing if not an abstraction of reality (whether a digital or a physical model), might one also move to a position where a scanned version of a building, or a streetscape, becomes an appropriate abstraction in its own right? Given that it is certainly possible to introduce new digital architecture within a scan, or to manipulate or even delete parts of the scan data, the scenarios for using such information collected in the field begin to present themselves. We will return in later sections to discuss particular examples of how laser scanning has in fact been used within study of the built heritage to serve technical, social and policy-based research and practice. What is interesting for us to consider at this juncture is how such a range of approaches might prove useful in attempting to scale the ladder of participation.

When engaging with a city, the occupants and users of that city might be presented with a range of opportunities through which they can express opinions, or through which they can begin to fully participate in decision making, genuinely influencing what those decisions are likely to be about. At a fairly basic level, this might involve being given the opportunity to review and perhaps comment on planning proposals put forward by a municipal authority (maybe in the form of city master plans), or by property developers or building owners, wishing to make modifications

Figure 4.3
Sample scene from laser scan in Elgin, Scotland. (Photo taken by author.)

or additions to the existing cityscape. The kinds of city model we have discussed above could certainly be used within such a context, where the models are used to present some kind of virtual simulation of how a city may look in the future, due to planned and designed changes. Where we begin to think, though, about digital technology being used to support higher and arguably more meaningful public participation, it can be useful to consider how such technology can be applied to simulate wider and perhaps more complex effects of new architecture (including both social and technical-environmental simulation, such as mobility, energy use, emissions, and so on), and how the technology can be used to support widespread debate among users of buildings, affected communities, experts and the municipal authorities themselves.

In that context, it is important that we reflect on some of the previously illustrated examples (city models), which exist on a spectrum of purely visual through to information-rich and simulation ready approaches to city modelling. One excellent, and relatively recent, example of such an information-rich and participation-enabled approach to digital planning has been developed and applied within the Swedish city of Gothenburg. 'Min Stad' is described by the city of Gothenburg as a digital bulletin board, within which residents are able to post ideas, perceptions and reactions to plans for the city, in a context which is intended to provoke lively and open debate. The system uses a 3D representation of

Gothenburg, which at first glance appears to have something in common with other similar online mapping platforms, such as Google Earth. The emphasis, though, which is placed on user engagement with the site is described as providing inspiration for city planners within Gothenburg,[2] although the system makes it quite clear that any kind of feedback loop, whereby users will be guaranteed some kind of response, is not part of the system. Nevertheless, the system does give a window into what is likely to be possible in the future, and what is in fact likely to become fairly standard as we try to move beyond pure consultation on planning ideas into a realm where the users and occupants of cities and designed areas are able to stimulate the ideas which then drive design. This is quite different from a situation where users and residents are simply asked to respond to ideas which have been suggested and stimulated by others.

In Calgary, Canada, work was completed to establish a framework for online participation in planning (planyourplace.ca, as noted in Hunter et al. 2012), specifically making use of Geographic Information Systems. Interestingly, the authors of that particular study also made a direct connection with the potential for using social media within planning (including both personal and professional platforms, such as Facebook and LinkedIn). Importantly, the authors make specific note of the urban planner being responsive to the idea of the citizen as a contributor to the planning development process, as opposed, presumably, to simply being responsive within more superficial consultation processes. With regard to the kinds of data which might form the basis for a system, Hunter et al. (2012) noted that information and specific skills were required to cover numerous fields:

- urban planning and transportation
- citizen participation
- Geographic Information Systems (GIS)
- Internet technologies
- social networking.

In addition to making reference again to Arnstein (1969), the authors here refer to the work of Carver (2003), who, apart from describing various approaches to e-democracy and e-participation, notes that we must also continue to be aware of the desire and need to extend beyond one-way consultation and move towards two-way communication between users and occupants of a city, where the nature of decision making becomes collaborative and inclusive, as opposed to being a top-down process. Hunter et al. ultimately propose a framework for online participatory planning where users of the system are able to access legal information (by-laws, policies) and use tools which enable collaborative participation to actually take place (for example, sketching tools, sharing of information, impact assessment). Crucially, they then propose that any such system must be tied to technical implementation, which in the case of their particular framework involves the use of visualisation (including both architectural visualisation – the visualisation of what buildings and streets look like – and data visualisation – abstracted visualisation of underlying information). Combined, one could argue that such an approach to participation will help to ensure that discussions take place on an informed basis, without that information unnecessarily constraining creativity and debate. With regard to visualisation itself, the authors proposed three main components for consideration:

- geographic data, which in the case of this particular paper included both topographic information and information pertaining to building footprints and land use data
- a suitable user interface, which enabled both the visualisation of information and access to social networking and other such collaborative tools, and
- access to external information services, which Hunter et al. suggest could include online geospatial tools, but in the case of architecture planning could presumably also include any cloud-based services, such as environmental simulation tools.

Crucially, the authors noted both from their own work and within other examples from the literature and previous research that there still remains a need for the development of digital tools which would enable migration towards online participation, but where it was possible for this to take place at higher levels of the participation ladder (Arnstein 1969). This aspect of the work undertaken in Calgary certainly connects back to the system described in Gothenburg, where there was a commitment on the part of planners to receive and reflect on suggestions submitted to the system. In that sense, one can recognise that there is at least an attempt being made to invite open discussion, as opposed to simply receiving comment on designs or ideas which are already well formed. Nevertheless, we are perhaps still some way short of realising forms of participation and engagement which extend quite high up Arnstein's ladder.

In later chapters, where we consider how digital tools and digital visualisation have been used within both research and practice, we will touch upon the notion of crowd sourced data. Although quite often mentioned in the context of smart cities and smart city technology, the techniques which underpin the use of crowd sourcing are becoming reasonably well established, and have been assisted in recent years through the prevalence of mobile technology and the use of apps which can update data in real time. The European Commission has supported a considerable amount of research and development work concerning the use of what are termed collective awareness platforms (or 'CAPS'). These tend towards recognition of existing online platforms, including the use of socially driven systems (social media) and technology which can be connected with building elements, objects and service utilities, perhaps through the use of sensor technology.

The European Commission noted that collective awareness platforms can support 'environmentally aware, *grassroots* processes and practices to *share knowledge*, to *achieve changes* in lifestyle, production and consumption patterns, and to set up more *participatory democratic processes*' (emphasis added).[3] It has been noted in the literature (Arniani et al. 2014) that one can actually regard the topic and practice of collective awareness as one which can help both individuals and communities to better understand the context (informed by the behaviour of others, and by the activities operating within systems) within which they are making their own decisions. Although it is by now a well-established concept, Arniani et al. (2014) also make the observation that whilst many such collective awareness platforms were originally established to deal with what might be termed environmental issues, these really need to be seen within the context of wider sustainability, which again returns us to the examples given in Gothenburg and Calgary, where participants and users of a system are able to access legal and economic information, thus ensuring that debate and decisions are undertaken within an informed context.

Another notable feature of the European approach to the use of online platforms to support community planning is the importance of user engagement. Although one could certainly argue that this can be measured using entirely objective approaches (e.g. the number of times an individual logs into the system, or the number or percentage of people within a community who actually use the system at any given time), one could also argue that an assessment of engagement with such a system should also include some deeper consideration of how users are able to go about suggesting, contributing and modifying either the system itself or the data contained within it.

Arniani et al. (2014) went on to think more widely about the ways in which digital awareness/participation platforms can be used to actually support the empowerment of individuals and communities. Among the key considerations was that of personal efficacy. This is of great importance as we consider planning and design of the built environment, and concerns the ways in which an individual might be able to feel that their opinions and actions actually hold the potential to change an outcome. In the context of Europe-wide studies this could of course refer to the ways in which an individual is able to contribute to mitigating climate change. Within the context of the design of the town or city, though, this may just as readily refer to the ways in which an individual is genuinely able to shape design and decision making. Although some of the examples which we will touch upon in later chapters, where we discuss the application of digital participatory tools to help study the provision of greenspace, or conservation within the built heritage, describe in quite clear terms how it is possible to support the engagement of end users in discussion and debate, this must surely have to go hand-in-hand with a wider recognition of how this fits within a wider societal system of governance and decision making. Arniani et al. (2014) suggest that the development of a technical platform must always go hand-in-hand with an appreciation of how this needs to interact with both formal (policy and regulation) and informal (motivations, values and beliefs) decision-making structures. This means in practical terms that the design of the technical system must take into account both policy and regulatory frameworks, as well as a clear consideration of the characteristics of likely end users. Likewise, participants in both the community and system design realms must recognise the importance of cross-discipline working, whereby it is understood that the potential benefits of developing a digital system to support participation are only likely to be realised where both technical and social aspects of the design problem have been fully recognised. On that basis, it is useful to consider individual case studies, and even descriptions of individual research projects, in this context. It is also interesting to note that, as the European research agenda has developed since the 2000s, we begin to see a gradual shift away from theoretical and even developmental research, which may in fact have some kind of practical base, towards work which is more obviously grounded in practice, and with the application of innovation in that practice. This means, in turn, that the importance of evaluation within such research and development becomes increasingly important, to trace whether the systems of technical, social and regulatory concerns can be demonstrated to be functioning in any recognisable sense.

Within this book, I have made mention of the complementary qualities of digital and analogue techniques, and the importance of recognising the need to find a way to form a bridge between each of the techniques and approaches. For example, we discussed those ways in which various researchers have explored methods through which hand drawings and sketches can be translated, either automatically or manually, into digital artefacts. One aspect of democratic technology which has emerged in recent years is that of 3D printing, which allows the designer or any other user of a digital model to produce a tangible physical version of objects which may have previously only existed in the digital domain. This is interesting from a philosophical perspective, in that it forces us to actively blur the distinction between digital and physical, and between abstract and real objects. From a practical perspective, though, the method and technology offer some important practical potential, not least within the fields of building survey and study of the built cultural heritage. Recent studies (Balletti, Ballarin and Guerra 2017) explore how the user of digital modelling software was able to first capture the geometrical reality of existing physical objects and then translate these into digital models. In the particular study by Baletti and colleagues, examples are offered of this data capture phase making use of laser scanning equipment. With reference to some of the preceding sections of this book, one could also have made use of photogrammetry, albeit while having to actively recognise the loss of geometrical sizing, even as proportional detail was retained, to some extent. Where the study is interesting from an architectural perspective is that the authors begin to suggest that the use of digitisation and subsequent 3D printing might actually offer a credible method through which people wishing to view and interact with objects from cultural heritage might be able to do so, without running the risk of damage to the original artefact or object. From a building survey perspective, one could argue that an obvious application of such technology in relation to existing buildings would be the potential use of 3D printing to reproduce details of a building (for example, intricate plaster mouldings) where doing so using traditional methods of surveying and fabrication might prove problematic. In terms of surveying processes, we could return to discussions of both laser scanning and photogrammetry, where the ability to capture geometrical detail without needing to be physically close to an object removes the need for both scaffolding and, in the case of laser scanning, adequate lighting within the building. With regard to the fabrication of objects and details within a building, one could certainly extend the discussion to recognise the difficulties which have been faced in many countries and regions with regard to a lack of availability of skilled traditional tradespeople.

Summary

In this chapter we have dealt with the subject of democratic access to digital technology. I would regard this as being a key strand of future research, and it should certainly be regarded as a key strand of future practice. We could certainly continue as an industry, operating within wider society, with the notion that collaboration with members of the public, and with end users of architecture, is something which is always likely to be driven by the industry itself. For example, where a major new piece of architecture is planned, one could be of the opinion that most forms of collaboration and engagement in that project are likely to come through invitations emanating from the design team themselves. After all, this has tended to be the model followed by planning and engagement projects, certainly in the UK, for many decades. Once something has been designed to a stage that it can be shown or displayed to people outside of the design team, that is the point at which you might consider asking a wider constituency what they 'think'. I would argue that the most valuable message which can be taken from this chapter is that we will increasingly reach a point where there are very few already constructed environments (certainly within open areas) which will not have already been explored, catalogued and debated to some extent by the wider public. This could have taken the form of a community undertaking their own 3D digital representations, or parts of that environment being represented through online forums, or simply through local interest in architecture or architectural heritage groups participating in more organised, if still informal, study of the local environment. As we move towards a greater use of online participation and engagement, and as we discuss further in the next chapter, there would therefore be a strong chance that online engagement will have already taken place, albeit not at the instigation of local public authorities or the local architecture and construction industry.

As an aside, in one of the earliest projects I was involved with that used visualisation, we were informed by a group of local residents participating in one of focus groups (designed to ensure that visualisations were geared towards following suggestions from members of the local community) that this was not the first such focus group they had attended. Indeed, the participants appeared light-hearted about the fact that their efforts to periodically discuss the future of their own neighbourhood in a collaborative creative and productive manner seemed each time to generate some kind of momentum before returning to square one. If we as a society can on a continuous basis recognise that useful discussion and debate are most likely taking place, and have most likely in fact already taken place and been recorded, represented and even already debated online, then perhaps we can avoid such a set of circumstances recurring quite so often in the future.

Notes

1. The Glasgow School of Art 'Digital Design Studio' has recently been undertaking ground-breaking work in collaboration with Historic Environment Scotland regarding digital recording of the built heritage, using both laser scanning and photogrammetry.
2. http://minstad.goteborg.se/minstad/index.do (accessed 24 April 2018).
3. https://ec.europa.eu/digital-single-market/en/programme-and-projects/caps-projects-fp7 (accessed 24 April 2018).

Chapter 5

Collaboration and participation

A key aspect of architectural visualisation which has been less explored in the literature has concerned the use of visualisation to engage end users and team members. This chapter draws on real examples from both research and industry to explore and understand how visualisation technology can in itself provide a mechanism to build consensus, stimulate debate, provoke discussion and shine a light on key issues.

In Chapters 2 and 3 we began to consider the implications of information modelling in terms of how this may have an effect on concepts of what we regard as maturity within the design team, and the ways in which embarking on a path towards the implementation of BIM will almost inevitably change how the design teams operate. Collaboration within a team can certainly be supported by the use of emerging digital tools and software. For example, recent work (Kim et al. 2015) demonstrated how the combined use of BIM to simulate the effects of design decisions can be particularly useful in terms of providing real-time feedback during the technical design stages, even when dealing with large-scale and highly complex projects. What is interesting about these more recent studies is that they move beyond an exploration of how to provide pieces of software, and consideration of how that software might be structured, to instead assess the implications of data and information provision on later decision making. It has also been heartening to see the emphasis being placed on numerous types of stakeholder within that decision-making process (Kourtit, Nijkamp and Stough 2017).

What has also been interesting in recent literature is the growing realisation that the use of BIM will in itself have an effect on behaviour and collaboration within a team. In some ways this reminds us of our earlier discussions of the use of digital design within architecture, where studies over many years have served to demonstrate that tools are being used within design (be they pencils, pens, CAD systems or virtual reality) that carry the potential to affect a design outcome, in much the same way that a musician's chosen instrument will be likely to have an effect on the music which emerges. Liu, van Nederveen and Hertogh (2017) have studied the ways in which BIM was perceived by professionals currently operating in the industry as having an effect on collaboration and collaborative practice. They propose that eight specific concepts were likely to significantly influence that collaboration:

- IT capacity
- technology management
- attitude and behaviour
- role taking
- trust
- communication
- leadership
- learning and experience.

In addition, that particular study indicated that some of these issues could be categorised as technology focused, with others being more concerned with people and process. The issue of learning and experience is interesting and relates back directly to our earlier discussions regarding the nature of the education process in our industry, part of which indeed has a technical focus, yet part of which is very much single discipline. Efforts are required to educate a discipline not just to understand their own core competencies, but also to develop the skills necessary to actively and productively collaborate with others in the wider design team.

In another recent study (Merschbrock and Munkvold 2015) it was observed that, in order to provide a collaborative environment which gained from the potential benefits of BIM, there was a need to recognise that factors affecting the successful implementation of new technology, and new working practices, are likely to come from individual, managerial and environmental areas, as well as from the technology itself. In the case of that particular study, which concentrated on the use of a collaborative environment for the design and delivery of a new hospital building, the team did in fact make use of BIM change agents, as well as ensuring that technical, contractual and educational processes were in place. From the perspective of our current discussion, considering the nature of effective collaboration, we are again drawn back to technical considerations, in that the change agents were technical BIM experts, and the training processes put in place concentrated on the technical mastery of software. Merschbrock and Munkvold (2015) noted that it was necessary in their particular case study project (which was on a very large scale) for the client to actually take an active role in the application of BIM, suggesting perhaps that the project context may actually have a significant effect on the behaviour and technical abilities of the wider design and construction team.

It is useful at this stage to consider some of these concepts in more depth. With regard to IT capacity, the authors of that particular study were able to identify that some issues of capacity were in fact not likely to be due to what they termed unsolved technical problems, but to relate as much to disconnections between technical systems which may exist within partner organisations, and the social systems which were then able to deal with those disconnections. For example, within the subject of technology management, it is also interesting to consider how management is required of the model creation process, and also how this is likely to be shared in practice. In another recent study (Oh et al. 2015) problems which can be encountered during cross-team collaboration included:

- loss of data
- difficulty in communication (presumably both face to face and mediated through technology)
- poor work efficiency.

The researchers were able to demonstrate how it was possible to develop new technical systems, as well as new workflows (incorporating all members of the design team), yet recognised that this technical approach to solving the issue of collaboration was only part of the solution. As with much of my own research, we cannot and should not avoid the problem that collaboration at its centre involves the working together of a team to reach a common goal. Although Oh et al. (2015) note that institutional and policy efforts may be required in order to overcome such problems and barriers to progress, it also appears likely that social and behavioural challenges will continue to exist unless we address deeper issues regarding discipline boundaries across the industry (Whyte 1999).

Using the appealing notion of the 'unorchestrated symphony', Merschbrock (2012) suggested that a barrier to realising some of the potential benefits of collaboration through digital design were not being realised by project participants due to the organisation of groups and processes failing to involve and integrate the implementation of new technologies. Merschbrock also felt that this limitation existed across organisations, although the challenge perhaps still exists of trying to deal with design and construction teams which are formed afresh for each new project. Nevertheless, there was some evidence that modelling was taking place in silos, leading to what the authors termed 'automation islands'. Attention was also drawn to the fact that much of the scholarship undertaken in relation to BIM has tended to focus on technical implementation, or development of standards which can then feed into the technical implementation of BIM. Elsewhere, Dossick and Neff (2011) noted that the very nature of BIM did in fact tend to structure conversations towards the exchange of 'explicit knowledge' and away from informal conversation, within which tacit knowledge could be exchanged, potentially leading to improved design team working and more effective design outcomes.

In some ways this is quite different from the way digital design tools were studied from a scholarship perspective in the 1970s and 1980s, where we can see a reasonable balance between understanding the technical development of new tools and the corresponding need to understand and appreciate the impact of these on design practice, and design outcomes. If we think again about some of our discussions regarding frameworks for the rollout and adoption of BIM in practice (Succar 2009), we almost inevitably start to think about the adoption of new workflows, which one must extend from the conceptual design stages through to the delivery of buildings, and in the fullness of time planning for the adoption of BIM during the life cycle of a building. With regard to the concepts noted, there did seem to be some evidence of there being a reluctance to initiate new workflows, due to a perception of the uneven benefits which might accrue.

With the adoption of any digital tools, whether these are within the realm of design or within a wider context of user engagement and user participation, we must recognise that new roles may begin to emerge within the design team (e.g. BIM coordinator), and that existing roles may change or evolve due to the introduction of new digital tools. There are connected issues of trust and communication within the design team that are also of great importance, with some evidence from the literature suggesting that the requirement to share information and data can, in some instances, lead to greater levels of trust between participants, although I might suggest that this would be worthy of further study in the coming years. Webber (2008) demonstrated that trust among group members can depend on key components:

- reliability, dependability and competence
- care, concern and emotional bonds.

What Webber was also able to demonstrate, though, was that these issues of trust were unlikely to manifest themselves immediately and in the case of her particular study required teams to work together for at least eight weeks. The importance of interpersonal relationships emerged as a strong component, and this in itself will require managing and nurturing in entirely different ways depending on the size and nature of a project, and perhaps even the prior working relationships of the design team, or the design team participants.

This usefully leads us to consider the notion of leadership within the digital design team, and opens a discussion about how collaboration and teamwork can in fact be facilitated. It is certainly possible to almost naturally move towards the consideration of a new role, where a third party, not previously a recognised participant with the design team (BIM manager, for example), can be introduced to oversee the design process. However, this does run the risk of introducing imbalance within a traditional design team process, and great care would be required to ensure that control and influence of design, which have been carefully nurtured by the design team from the conceptual stages, do not in any way become a technocratic process as we approach the construction phases.

Within the context of this book, where we are examining the influence of digital tools upon collaboration, we can also consider how such tools could be brought to the design team to help facilitate collaboration taking place. In the case of some recent research (Leon et al. 2014) this included the use of digital visual design tools (in the case of that particular study, larger-scale interactive digital tables), combined with the use of directed design protocols, helping to ensure that the media being used to facilitate collaboration did not undermine the benefits of traditional design processes. In this way, it becomes possible to understand how 'leadership' within the team can still exist, but we can also begin to appreciate how digital technology can be useful to ensure wider participation from all design team members. That is, the design team is only going to operate as a team with participation, at appropriate junctures, from all team members.

If we then return to the notion and subject of *learning* and *experience*, I would again argue that this is going to have both technical and social or behavioural components. From a technical perspective, I am reminded of early industry focused events concerning the implementation of digital architecture, and BIM in particular. Although some time tended to be given over to the technical demonstration of software, the entirely appropriate emphasis placed on the challenge of implementing BIM across an industry (at the time, by the BIM Task Group) was on behavioural change. That is, learning how to use software which is capable of storing information within architectural models is a necessary step, but it is arguably one which should be addressed by many firms through the employment of recent graduates, or through some modest upskilling of existing staff. What is going to be more difficult, and what could arguably be best addressed through the combination of experience and education, will be the challenge of collaborating in a manner which has not been experienced in the past.

With regard to the participation of end users, and certainly since the 1960s, we have seen a significant growth in the body of work dealing with the relationships which exist between people and the constructed environment. Often studied within the field of environmental psychology, this has seen the development of methodologies to help support engagement with end users, as well as research data helping designers and the wider society to understand the complex relationship between people, buildings and their environment, with an appreciation that the relationships and influences inherently run in both directions. That is, we influence our environment and surroundings, and we are likewise influenced by that environment (this may be in terms of educational attainment, standard of living, wellbeing, resource consumption and suchlike). In response to the suggestion that failings of public and user engagement were an intrinsic part of 'participation', Lawrence (1982) presented a forceful argument that any limitations should be identified as being part of the methods and approaches employed by researchers and professionals, rather than being a core problem of participation in itself. Whilst the purpose of participation in design might well be understood and appreciated (to bring added value to the design and hopefully produce designs which better meet the needs of users), the reality might well be little more than an A/B choice between options, if users are not involved throughout. This is not to say, as argued by Lawrence, that designers and planners somehow cede responsibility for design and innovation, but rather that methods should be found through which users can be helped to provide 'behavioural' information, which can usefully and meaningfully inform the development of a design. In this sense, we start to think of a deeper or better-informed design brief, rather than falling into the clutches of 'design by committee', or a process whereby an inspirational design is reduced in ambition due to unhelpful limitations being placed on creativity. Lawrence draws on the work of Broadbent (1988) in categorising methodologies under the broad headings of:

- behaviourists (Lawrence preferred 'determinism', referring to measurement, assessment and prediction)
- phenomenologists (Lawrence pointing to a lack of design-led phenomenology studies, although this has to some extent been addressed in the intervening years)
- collectivists (design as a collective activity, with users 'as' designers).

Elsewhere, Broadbent (1988) himself describes the characteristics of the lone designer, the design team working across multiple locations (described, from the early 1970s as a 'synthetic' team, rather than 'virtual') and a 'face-to-face' group. Broadbent argued that the synthetic team would typically be able to identify 'random' errors, to remember information, to produce a greater volume of ideas than the individual and to avoid duplication of effort. It seems obvious that to realise such benefits and advantages requires some degree of management and intentionality. With regard to face-to-face meetings, Broadbent highlights the possibility of participants being able to react continuously to each other, and to ideas as they emerge. He argues that there is the potential in such a setting for what he describes as an 'assembly' effect, where collective ideas build on one another to ensure that the final design ideas are of a higher quality (in whatever sense) than those produced by the individual. Again, I would tend to argue that assessment of what constitutes a higher quality of idea is open to debate, and is likely to be affected by the participants and by the design intention.

Reflecting on my own research, although the studies have tended to shy away from collective design (aspects of our work regarding greenspace leaned towards citizen panels), many studies intent on capturing something of the human experience of urban environments have tended to utilise methods which might be regarded as both deterministic (e.g. contingent rating, choice experiments) and drawing on phenomenology (e.g. studies of the experience of being 'in' a virtual space, or studies concerning the impact of the built environment on the senses). It was argued (Lawrence 1982) that the creativity of a designer should not be lessened by the use of participation in design, but that they need to add new methods of working ('new capacities') to allow for participation, and information emanating from that participation, to enrich the design. I would caution against automatically transferring this finding to cover a design 'team' composed of different disciplines. The additional issue of a multi-faceted 'design team' having to interact with a client group adds further complexity, and will require new professional and interpersonal skills.

Recent research (Fonseca et al. 2016) has explored how the use of digital technology can be valuable as a means to connect with end users, whilst recognising that the use of technology in such a context itself carries the potential to alter the ways in which the design team may operate. That particular study, which engaged with a user group in Mexico, also explored the implications of using mobile sketching technology in the field, and how this might affect the educational process and curriculum. The use of digital technology, including augmented reality applications, certainly seems to have a positive effect on student engagement and student motivation. It should also be noted that this was undertaken alongside more traditional methods of visual representation, including sketching and the use of photography, supporting an integrated approach to the use of new technologies.

Democratic engagement in planning and design

Much of my own research over the past 20 years has involved the use of various methods which might be collectively regarded as supporting public engagement in planning and design. Those studies were actually quite disparate in terms of their apparent overriding subject matter (technical building conservation, streetscape design, access to greenspace, urban mobility), yet all contained a central strand which utilised visual and often digital techniques to facilitate dialogue and discussion and to channel collective opinion in ways which could be used to positively aid decision making. In this sense, it can be argued that the research was very much in keeping with a tradition of studies dating back to the 1960s (Sanoff 2011).

One overall conclusion we can draw from this is that the use of digital visualisation appears to hold two areas of potential, these being to convey and contain information in ways which are not possible using analogue techniques, coupled with the possibility of supporting and encouraging engagement. Through the (re)presentation of environments, settings and buildings with which a person might be familiar, there might emerge the possibility of fresh insights. This point has been argued (Spence 2007,

Figure 5.1
Laser scan of landscape, with building. (Image produced by Dr Marianthi Leon.)

Tufte 2001) within the field of information visualisation, and resonates within architecture.

Over the course of the last two decades, I have been personally involved with, and in some cases led, research which dealt with a number of these issues. Although the context and specific focus of each of the studies varied in terms of method from project to project, a common thread running between them has been the use of visualisation to act as the main method of communication between researchers and research participants. Using visualisation and visual methods to communicate what were actually quite complex research studies meant that my colleagues and I were able to undertake studies which involved a very wide range of participants from a wide range of backgrounds.

The subjects under consideration within the studies ranged from the design of streets through to the provision of parks and urban greenspace, and more recently involved the study of built heritage and the ways in which people might care about their personal connections with that built heritage. However, although it is possible to try to somehow condense these experiences into one, the reality is that they took place over the course of a long enough time period for technology to develop, both in terms of the visualisation tools and in terms of how we were able to communicate these between ourselves and with research participants. So, in the very early studies it felt as if we had achieved something very significant if we managed to do something simple like putting an image on the website. Whilst the underlying research methodology (often taken from environmental economics or environmental psychology) was well established, the way in which this could be rolled out against a rapidly developing Internet, where the Internet itself was still not pervasive, was a real challenge. In the following sections, I try to deal with some of the technical challenges which faced the research, and although the technology varies from example to example, the underlying themes which I identify still hold even within research and public engagement studies taking place in the present time.

Image manipulation

My own personal first experiences of using visualisation within applied research concerned the issue of image manipulation. It is interesting to reflect upon the extent to which the technically time-consuming and inaccessible equipment of that era has in time given way to methods of working which make those initial attempts at visualisation now seem rather archaic.

One study, undertaken in the mid-1990s and concerning the conservation of stone buildings in Scotland (mainly granite, in the case of my own work), considered the ways in which people perceive changes to the appearance of elevations over time. The study followed work by a colleague involving pairs of near-identical buildings in 'paired' studies. In plain terms, subtle but important differences in the quality of the stonework gave rise to perceptions of age, quality and aesthetic preference. This was easiest to achieve at the time using sections of tenement or terraces, where the stone of one part had been cleaned and other sections left untouched.

Previous research had used a manual approach to image editing, in that the study required that visual differences were controlled to ensure that *only* the stone differed. Therefore, the research needed to ensure that windows, doors and so on were constant between photographs (as a seagull or an attractive set of curtains might sway opinion!). The manual approach involved taking two photographs, manually cutting the windows, doors and other details from one, and then attaching these over the second. The outcomes were actually very effective, albeit requiring a certain amount of trial and error in terms of the original photography (exposure, print quality, size, control of keystoning and so on). Examples from the studies can be found in Andrew, Young and Tonge (1994).

It is worth noting that this particular series of projects was also my first contact with tilt shift photography using architectural 'shift' lenses. Tilt shift photography is of particular interest in that the lenses are designed to help the photographer overcome issues of keystoning using optics, as opposed to what may perhaps be more normal nowadays, the use of digital photograph manipulation afterwards. Having said that, younger readers of this book may struggle to fully understand my description of the mass disappointment of receiving 36 prints from the chemist, only to find that 25 are completely unusable. I referred in Chapter 4 to the use of tilt shift photography and some of the technical challenges, which in themselves have become desirable features for completely unintentional reasons.

The process of photographic manipulation which was undertaken within this initial building conservation study brings our attention to two particular and equally important factors. The first of these remains significant within all visualisation research, and refers to the appropriate use of technology, where that technology adds something demonstrable to either the research methodology or the research outcomes. In the case of this particular study, there appeared to be some clear technical benefits to using digital photographic editing, as opposed to manual approaches. These included the ability to scale parts of the building to match entirely different images (for example the content of windows, or the material used for roof coverings). Relating to the point I made in the preceding paragraph, digital manipulation undertaken by the researcher inevitably gives the researcher far more control over the characteristics of the overall image. For example, the researcher is able to control the contrast, brightness and exposure settings, in addition to removing imperfections within an image. In the case of the particular piece of research being referred to, this had both positive and negative implications, in that the intention was to explore the reaction of research participants to the appearance of actual buildings. The researcher could possibly have started to manipulate the colouration and appearance of surface characteristics, and although I did not personally undertake such processes, these could arguably have been explored in further work.

The other aspect of technical visualisation research which emerged as a major factor in that study was that of actually extracting material from the computer system, once the digital manipulation had been undertaken. That is, in the mid-1990s it was not yet common for consumer-level equipment to allow the researcher to print images using normal photographic paper, or to a standard which was comparable to colour images printed using traditional photographic printing techniques. Therefore, in the case of that particular research, I had to resort to spending reasonably large amounts of the research budget on a process known as dye-sublimation, where the printing process was undertaken by others, and at a fee. Nevertheless, the actual message to be taken from this is that the technical process embarked on by the visualisation researcher was certainly aimed at exploring the extent of the software and hardware capabilities being used, but required significant and, importantly, potentially invasive contributions from others, where those parties were completely external to the research process. This has been a characteristic of a number of studies with which I have been involved, where exciting and innovative aspects of the research process may in fact require explanation of the method itself, in addition to using the method to explore responses to research questions.

Viewing and rating images online

One study which was undertaken as part of the initial building conservation doctoral research concerned the use of environmental economics. In my own early work, which concerned the ways in which and the extent to which people place a value on the buildings which surround them, I elected to use a method called contingent valuation. As a methodology, contingent valuation has been studied extensively within research programmes and applied reasonably widely within practice. From the perspective of a research participant, the method appears quite simple

Collaboration and participation

Figure 5.2
Keystoning effect. (Photo taken by author.)

Collaboration and participation

Figure 5.3
Keystoning effect (after digital correction). (Photo taken by author.)

in that, in addition to being asked questions about prior knowledge and their own demographics, the main questions within contingent valuation study revolve around the likes of 'how much would you be willing to pay to see[.]happen?' and 'how much would you need to receive in order to accept that [something you disagree with] happens'? For my doctoral studies, I chose to undertake contingent valuation work in the field. Therefore, I had no need to show people images of the buildings being studied, as the study was positioned right in the middle of the environment under consideration (people could look at the actual buildings being discussed).

From a visualisation perspective, though, one distinct limitation of that approach was an inability within the method to present the visual impact of new scenarios to the respondent group. Therefore, in a piece of slightly later research which involved the study of streetscape design (the study was instigated by Professor Seaton Baxter with Scottish Enterprise), we as a research team decided to use a combination of two technical approaches within the method, both of which were geared towards the visual presentation of streetscape change to our respondent group. To provide some kind of background, the study had emerged from a realisation that towns across Scotland were periodically spending money and resource upgrading streetscapes (for example, benches, bins, signs, landscaping, trees), on the basis that such work would lead to a longer-term sustainability of the street and require less in the way of intervention in the future. The reality in many instances, though, was that the intervention seemed to be rejected and underused by the local population or appeared to solve problems which didn't exist, or signal those which were actually quite pleasant. One could of course argue that the long-term quality of streetscape enhancements is going to be part of a far wider, and far more complex, scenario and system, and that is indeed something which my colleagues and I have written about over the years. Nevertheless, from a visualisation perspective we can learn some other important lessons from the experience of the streetscapes study.

The first of these concerns the use of three-dimensional architectural modelling to engage end users in a process of discussion and debate. For this particular study, and in the other examples which I will run through, we tended towards the use of modelling techniques which were geared towards the visual representation of objects (buildings and streets), as opposed to using information rich modelling approaches such as those which would be available using Geographical Information Systems.[1] Typically utilising a combination of geometrical modelling software normally used to assist in draughtsmanship, combined with an intensive use of software geared towards image rendering, we were able to produce

Collaboration and participation

Figure 5.4 (top) Photograph of Castlegate, Aberdeen. (Photo taken by author.)

Figure 5.5 (left) Image taken from 3D Max model of Castlegate, Aberdeen. (Image produced by Stephen Scott.)

virtual 'versions' of streetscapes, where we were able to closely control what was represented within the space and to alter configurations. The research design we used is related in some ways to that of contingent valuation, but we asked the respondents to express a preference between any two options presented to them (choice experiments). Each 'choice' in the case of our research was a combination of visualisations emerging from the modelling work and some wider contextual information (e.g. local taxes, etc.).

At the time we were undertaking this particular research, we were not yet at the stage of being able to collect site data using laser scanning technology, so the models themselves relied on a combination of established Ordnance Survey information (providing data about horizontal distances) and estimation of building and feature heights from photographs and site visits. The real value of the model, though, which became apparent once we embarked on the research itself, was the ability to insert, delete, move or otherwise adjust features within the streetscape, responding directly to views and opinions put forward during focus group and other discussions within the research. It was this ability to ensure that visualisation actually responded to socially driven data emerging from the research which then ensured the method became one of the predominant approaches within my own research for the next 15 years. Looking at the images now, whilst one can be critical of the visual realism of the rendering and the materials, the models themselves still stand up to scrutiny and gave the research which emerged from that study a genuine coherence.

As has been mentioned elsewhere, I would strongly argue, within the context of studies like those described in this chapter, that having a clear philosophical basis for the studies is certainly as important as, and should be regarded as an equal to, any technical considerations. Although we have indeed, as a research team, published papers which deal in the main with the development of the technical approaches used for the visualisation work, the larger studies themselves relied quite extensively on trying to determine the motivations, preferences, needs and ideas of (at the very least) representative members of the local community, or local formal decision makers. In the case of our research looking particularly at streetscapes, this actually involved a complete and distinct stage of work completed before any visualisation was designed or undertaken. For example, we attempted to determine physical features within the existing urban landscape which would be likely to lead to later survey responses which referred to particularly unattractive aspects of the built environment. We spent quite considerable time trying to catalogue the range of street furniture which was already present within the city we were studying. As an aside, this gave further fuel to the view that the city had in fact seen upgrading of the streetscape on a periodic basis, in the sense that it was quite possible to identify the earliest through to the latest litter bins currently in place. From a visualisation perspective, one of the important outcomes from that particular study was that it allowed the visualisation work to begin, with regard to the modelling of particular objects and, to some extent, in relation to the selection of and rendering of streetscape coverings.

The second major qualitative study which was undertaken involved interaction with a range of possible respondent groups who were perceived by the research team to have an interest in the study and the subjects being considered by the research. These included local residents, members of the wider general public, and representatives of the local decision-making team (from the local municipal authority). Taking the form of a series of structured focus groups, this method has become a common feature of much of the research which has been undertaken by the research team in subsequent years. It was felt, in the case of our study of streetscapes, that the method was particularly useful in terms of being able to identify and define 'scenarios' which could then be visualised within the research design. Examples might include the remodelling of a square as a pedestrian thoroughfare, or the reorganisation of street furniture in particular configurations, or the reintroduction of vehicular traffic.

The main intention when undertaking such qualitative studies is to move beyond a situation where the respondent and participant in research is involved simply as a passive observer, or simply as a participant required to answer certain very specific questions, which have been designed by the research team. Although it is probably impossible to ensure that many hundreds of respondents are able to participate as fully as is possible in a small group setting, or in a one-to-one interview, by dedicating time and resources to public engagement in the early stages of research we can at least try to ensure that the visualisations have been altered to respond to issues which have been raised by the respondent group, and will in some meaningful way reflect the concerns about and also the knowledge of a particular space, which are only likely to be apparent to those working in, working with or living in an area on a day-to-day basis. There are some wider considerations within such research design, not the least of which reside within the discussion of the generation of original ideas, or original scenarios, which have maybe not been envisaged in the past.

Quite apart from the challenge of modelling an urban streetscape so that it could be then considered by respondents who were familiar with the 'real' space, an even more challenging aspect of research concerned

Collaboration and participation

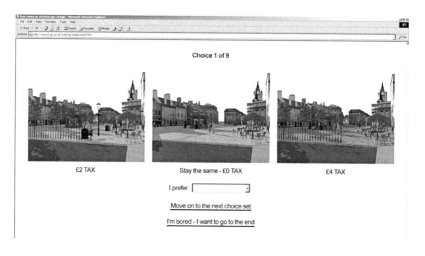

Figure 5.6
Excerpt
from online
survey. (Image
produced by
Stephen Scott.)

our desire to run a number of experiments over the Internet. Although we were aware of there being a precedent for this having been undertaken elsewhere (Bishop, Wherrett and Miller 2001), this aspect of the research raised questions which are still valid today, these being related to accessibility and an ability for further research to reach an appropriate respondent group. Although in the middle of the city centre, the location was certainly not among the most economically affluent areas. Therefore, in the context of this particular research, there was a genuine need and desire to ensure that the research was not limited to either interested academics or respondents who were simply able to participate because they owned or had access to a computer and a reliable Internet connection. Results from the studies themselves were reported widely, and the research design and data analysis formed a very significant part of the doctoral work undertaken by my colleague Anne-Marie Davies (2004). The lessons which we learned regard the use of technology which was appropriate to serve the needs of the research. There was a need to balance a desire to be technically inventive and exploratory against an equal desire to ensure accessibility and an ability to participate in the research among a wide constituency. These remain concerns which I and other visualisation researchers need to consider in every project.

If one can draw a practical message from this particular study of streetscapes which would apply to most visualisation led projects, it would be connected with compromise from a technical perspective, to ensure that the project and research aims are still met. There was a need, for example, to ensure that the images being posted online were of a sufficiently small file size that respondents using dial-up Internet connections were able to download them in a timely manner. Although we might think that such concerns have now been overcome due to increasing Internet speeds, this is probably not the case in reality. Much of our recent visualisation work, which I will touch upon later (particularly regarding digital recording of the built heritage), has tended to generate massive file sizes, meaning that corresponding users and collaborators not only require fast Internet connections, but also access to computer equipment which is able to deal with the datasets. On this note, we need to return to our earlier discussion of analogue versus digital techniques, to ensure that we are making the best use of digital visualisation where and when it is actually required.

Greenspace – 'real' growth and connections with social science

One slightly later study in which I participated concerned urban greenspace, located in various cities and city regions across Europe. Although the underlying methodology utilised by my team certainly extended our previous experience working on streetscapes, this particular study widened the scope of the visualisation quite considerably. It not only looked at reasonably small and confined open spaces, but also included consideration of much more expansive areas of greenspace. It also involved collaboration with researchers and practitioners who were applying methods from Geographical Information Systems (GIS), qualitative approaches to community engagement and the use of visualisation which was driven by information as well as by aesthetic considerations.

Given the scale of the environments which were under consideration during this particular project, we decided to follow an established research path. That is, visualisations could, to some extent, be derived from attempting to model the existing environment. However, most of the research questions and research challenges actually related to issues which were going to be raised by respondents and affected communities and community groups.

The underpinning methods which we decided to use in this particular study were again taken from environmental economics (led by Davies) and required participants in the visualisation studies to 'rate' the scenes and scenarios presented to them (Laing et al. 2008). The focus groups and discussions which were undertaken by the research team with people who lived near and used the greenspaces we had selected for study were used to determine the features, characteristics and attributes of each site which might lead to changes in behaviour or perception. For example, discussions touched upon issues of perceived safety, usefulness, how the parks were used at different times of the day and in the evening, and any other issues which focus group members wished to raise. This allowed us within the context of the visualisation to ensure that we were concentrating on the visual presentation of those attributes and those issues which had been raised within the discussions.

The studies themselves, which were widely disseminated through published academic work, used a paper-based survey technique. Learning from our experience while looking at streetscapes, the feeling of the researchers was that people may in fact be more willing and more able to participate in the research if they were not required to specifically log in to a website. It is interesting to note, perhaps, that the methods used today for public engagement in relation to the planning and design of our cities still quite often use paper-based materials to support engagement, despite what one might regard as the widespread availability of online techniques. The studies undertaken by my colleagues and me in relation to greenspace attempted to ensure that the 'burden' on participants was kept to a minimum. This meant that, in the main, people simply had to tell us in relation to scenarios presented to them whether they felt the scenes were attractive or unattractive, whether they felt the scenarios appeared safe, and whether they would be likely to visit that particular area of greenspace under the condition shown. In combination with some additional demographic information which was collected, this allowed the research team to identify any connections which existed between demographics, attributes, location and other such variables.

One could certainly argue that the use of this kind of visualisation (using printed images and requiring the respondents themselves to make a connection between visualisation and any additional information which is presented to them) goes only part of the way to creating a holistic environment within which researchers and the respondents can make informed decisions. As I mentioned earlier, in relation to my own doctoral studies, there seemed to be some value in undertaking fieldwork within the actual physical environments which were being studied. In the case of my doctoral studies, though, we were really dealing with a single variable. That is, do people agree with the cleaning of stone facades? Other than avoiding undertaking such studies in the rain, there was little philosophical reason to avoid undertaking the studies at any particular time of day or year.

In complete contrast to this, our study of greenspace was quite explicit in that we were interested in how people may perceive the spaces at different times of the day or during different seasons, or how perception might be affected by issues such as lighting or the provision of facilities. This meant that whilst the participants and any studies were arguably somewhat distanced from the greenspace under consideration,

Figure 5.7
Photograph of greenspace area. (Image produced by Stephen Scott.)

Figure 5.8
Image from 3D Max model of same area. (Image produced by Stephen Scott.)

the research design did nevertheless make a reasonable attempt to represent spaces under a range of conditions. I would tend to compare and contrast this approach with many other studies using similar techniques from environmental economics, almost regardless of the subject matter being studied, where the context for decisions and responses would be presented within the research design using text only, as I have alluded to on a number of occasions in the book. I feel it is important further researchers and practitioners give due consideration to the appropriateness of when to use visualisation and when instead to use an alternative approach (for example on-site studies, photographic studies, or text-based survey techniques). For this particular piece of research, we believed that it was important to derive and develop some control over the aesthetic aspect of the greenspace being studied, and thus the aesthetic impact which was going to be considered by respondents. One could of course undertake a similar study where one solely used text to describe scenarios, although this would need to be matched to any particular research direction being followed. Indeed, some important and ground-breaking work undertaken in Edinburgh (Aspinall et al. 2010) used text-based descriptions and representations of greenspace, recognising that there are significant difficulties when attempting to recognise variability in relation to seasonal, atmospheric and other such environmental changes in an area or scene.

As mentioned earlier, the study of greenspace was also one of the first opportunities I had to personally interact with and use information-based visualisation techniques, as opposed to the geometrical and aesthetic techniques typically used within architecture and building. What was interesting, and to some extent this has a great deal in common with my preceding discussion about matching the method with the research philosophy of any particular study, is that the information-based techniques were used in quite different ways, and to help find answers to quite different questions.

The first of these techniques which is worth discussing here is that of Geographic Information Systems (GIS), which has been used and developed by planners and geographers for many years, often to address questions related to the spatial layout of landscapes, towns and transport systems. Although the subject matter of this book concerns participation and engagement in architectural design, many of the underlying features of GIS draw one's attention towards the capabilities and structure of building information modelling (BIM), in that the metadata associated with objects and structure is contained within the model and is certainly as important as the aesthetics. One key difference which must be recognised between the historical development of GIS and that of BIM is that GIS is spatially driven, as opposed to having a focus on the characteristics of objects contained within an architectural structure. Having said that, any distance between the two is gradually eroding due to there being obvious benefits to combining GIS and BIM in the future.

Within the context of our study concerning greenspace, we utilised GIS (under the leadership of Professor David Miller and his team at the James Hutton Institute, Aberdeen) to explore the relative accessibility of greenspace within cities. In the case of Aberdeen, this served to highlight important socio-economic issues which would arguably have been difficult to determine through the use of non-visual and non-information-driven approaches. One major outcome of that part of the study (Laing et al. 2006) was to show that there seemed to be a disconnection between the accessibility of greenspace where visitors were limited to the use of public transportation and the availability of suitable public transport routes connecting areas of the city which were known to have a very low incidence of car ownership or poor access to mobility options other than public transport ('how accessible is your greenspace?'). Although this issue may have come up, one could argue that it would be more likely for a response to focus instead on greenspace with which they were familiar, or greenspace which they were actually able to visit at the moment. It also reminds one of the seminal study by John Snow (discussed in Chapter 2) which used map overlays of London and was thus able to identify (through reasoning and utilisation of visualised data) unforeseen connections between people, location, water and the spread of disease.

In this case, the use of an information visualisation technique led directly to a study which was ostensibly concerned with greenspace and urban parks having much wider social implications, and wider implications for how a greenspace in a city like Aberdeen can be managed for the benefit of all. This does in fact relate directly to connected transport studies undertaken within the city,[2] and the use of visual approaches to present the results is arguably far more accessible and understandable than simply presenting a range of statistics.

The second area of information-driven visualisation which I would like to discuss relates to the approach taken by Mambretti (2007) and her colleagues, at ETH Zurich, with regard to the visualisation of planting, landscaping and growth in greenspace areas. Within the visualisation studies undertaken in Aberdeen, our emphasis was very much on attempting to present a visualisation of the space which to a great extent would show what the space looks like under certain conditions. We gave no consideration to how changes in environmental conditions might actually affect the plants and trees existing within the greenspace at a given time. Therefore, although two of the areas of greenspace we considered were located next to reasonably busy roads, the effects of pollution on the plants even at the periphery of the greenspace were not necessarily reflected within the visualisations or the models. In quite sharp contrast to this, the team at ETHZ concentrated for part of their work on an area of greenspace which was located immediately above a major motorway route into the centre of Zurich. Therefore, the visualisation technique which was adopted by them afforded a direct consideration of prevailing environmental conditions, including pollutants and, for example, the direction and intensity of sunlight, to virtually 'grow' trees and plants within the greenspace model. Again I would relate back to the preceding section, where we identified how the distance between GIS and BIM has become increasingly narrow over the years. Likewise, the approach we would take nowadays within Aberdeen to modelling areas of greenspace would be quite different from that taken a number of years ago. For example, now that we have access to scanning equipment which would enable us to record the greenspace under different conditions, our tendency might be to record the greenspaces in different seasons, thus providing highly detailed and accurate models of the spaces when trees are in leaf, and the effects on visibility, daylighting and perceived accessibility during different parts of the year. One of the benefits of the approach taken by Mambretti (2007), and one which cannot be understated in terms of its value to the research, is that the underlying models at no time regard the greenspaces as being static, or space which was unlikely to change over time. Of course, and as with any predictive model, the underlying assumptions inserted by the modeller would require some basis in reality, but a strong connection between architectural design, modelling and ecology (as was the case in that particular study) brings huge benefits to the modelling and visualisation processes and outcomes.

Image sorting

The overall subject matter of this book concerns the use and application of digital participation in architectural design and planning of our towns and cities. Nevertheless, it is very important that we do not lose sight of the fact that there are many techniques which have been used for many generations which make no use whatsoever of computer visualisation, and which perfectly serve the purpose for which they were originally designed. In all of the visualisation research with which I have been involved, one must remain conscious of the fact that digital visualisation and digital modelling are simply new tools in the toolbox, and should not be regarded as methods which are inevitably going to supersede analogue techniques. In fact one could go further and say again that we must always try to match the range of available techniques with the job which is actually in hand.

One excellent example of this came within a study undertaken by a team at my own university, which concerned the connection and accessibility of some key urban locations in the middle of the city centre. In one particular study, led by my colleague Tony Craig, we used the sorting of printed photographs to investigate the issues of perceived safety, attractiveness, familiarity and so on. The technique involves presenting research participants with any reasonably large collection of photographs, and then asking them to sort them using whichever criteria they preferred.

Figure 5.9
Photograph sorting study. (Photo taken by author.)

In most cases people would begin by trying to sort the images on the basis of where they felt the photographs had been taken, for example images in a particular park, a particular street or a particular square, and so on. The results of this research study were fascinating and uncovered some issues and factors within the city which we had not predicted. For example, some quite small areas of open space were not regarded in a uniform manner, with some parts perceived to be dangerous and other parts which were actually geographically very close by regarded as accessible and attractive. In the case of one particular area (known locally as 'The Green'), which in terms of layout at least is a remnant of medieval Aberdeen, clear evidence emerged that the local occupants of Aberdeen, who had stayed here for many years, were actually quite unfamiliar with that part of the city centre. As an aside, it has been interesting in the few years since we undertook this research to observe a range of initiatives being undertaken within that particular part of the city centre, including the introduction of a home zone and some examples of street art, to try not only to encourage physical accessibility but also to encourage people to actually travel to and visit the space (these two things not necessarily being one and the same).

Figure 5.10
Street art in
The Green (as
part of the
Nuart festival).
(Photo taken by
author.)

Heritage studies

An important technical method which has emerged in recent years as being vital to our work regarding user engagement and participation in design has been that of high-definition laser scanning. Laser scanning is often portrayed as a technical approach which allows us to record the current condition of environments, buildings, landscapes and so on. My own department initially purchased laser scanning equipment on the basis that it would over time begin to replace our use of traditional landscape surveying techniques. Such techniques are designed and widely used within architecture and building to set out a construction site prior to building work commencing. A key difference with laser scanning, as I am describing it in this particular section, is that the technique is typically used to record the existing environment, as opposed to having its main use in terms of setting out what is likely to happen in the future. Within my own areas of interest (which cover both construction and built heritage) it has been interesting to note how laser scanning has managed to gain a foothold in recording the progress of often very large construction projects, including transport mega-projects, as well as increasingly finding a place in the digitisation of our built heritage. It is the latter of these two applications which will be discussed in this section.

There has been a significant growth in recent years in the use of digital methods to capture, record and represent the built heritage. This has given rise to many examples of research activity whereby aspects of that heritage are documented, often in ways which could facilitate their inclusion in new design work, wider virtual city models, or as part of conservation work. One naturally wishes to explore the nature and significance of such work, in terms of fabric conservation, while bearing in mind that the record is an abstraction of reality, albeit one which may be aesthetically convincing and geometrically accurate. However, the potential benefits of holding such data in a form which documents and can portray the built heritage to expert and non-expert audiences alike are notable, and could in themselves constitute a useful tool to further democratise the heritage conservation movement. Of course, one must always be mindful of Magritte's (1928) warning to avoid a confusion between real objects and visual representations of those objects.

Laser scanning has developed into a standard tool for recording cultural heritage and is applicable to archaeological assignments in relation to heritage preservation, interpretation and presentation (Hakonen, Kuusela and Okkonen 2015) and to architectural heritage (Al-kheder, Al-shawabkeh and Haala 2009, Lambers et al. 2007). Its importance lies in monitoring sites of historic significance and context, thus keeping a record of their evolution within time. In the case of urban integrated monuments and sites, particular care is required, not only for restoration or preservation purposes but most importantly for understanding the impact of changes in the city for the relevant heritage. As a result, heritage visualisation can acknowledge the relationship of monuments with the city, leading to the promotion of decision making in relation to place making and the genius loci[3] (Norberg-Schulz 1980).

The emerging technologies (including scanning, photogrammetry, location-tagged imaging and social data recording) have become more affordable in recent years, to the point that their use in practice is now less limited by issues of funding. However, harnessing the value of that technology to ensure that the data collected is of greatest use to society requires the development of further technologies to support the combined storage and presentation of data, and the development of technical workflows to support widespread engagement. This engagement extends across different types of community, for example those defined by geography, interest and organised in both formal and informal ways. Engagement carries great significance for cultural heritage in relation to place making, urban and individual identity and as a way to connect and enhance social relations and practice.

The studies used in this section as examples of heritage visualisation draw on various pieces of research, which have distinct research questions and research objectives. The first study concerned the visual recording and representation of a collection of heritage buildings located in the Faeroes, which were initially modelled as part of a very small-scale study looking at connections between Scandinavian architecture and examples of buildings located in Aberdeen. The research was extended as a direct result of us feeling that the initial 3D digitisation failed to capture the experience of visiting the site itself. That is, we were able to develop 3D models which gave a representation of the geometry and layout of the site, but which failed to convey to the user of that model the experience of actually walking between the buildings themselves, and being able to relocate on the waterfront after navigating the narrow spaces left between the timber clad buildings. Therefore the first study dealt to a great extent with the experience of moving between buildings, and to some extent reminds us of the work undertaken by Cullen (1961) and others on the importance of movement, awareness of our surroundings, and our awareness of how those surroundings change as we move through an environment.

As noted, the initial research undertaken to generate this particular 3D digital model was a fairly pragmatic piece of work, which was primarily used to help celebrate cultural connections between two quite separate locations. The towns involved were 'twinned' (Torshavn and Aberdeen), and the intention behind the research was to effectively communicate something of the architecture and character of the existing built environment, consisting of landscapes and buildings in quite specific coastal and headland locations. It is useful to reflect again on the modelling process which was undertaken as part of that project. Referring for a moment to the use of visualisation within marketing, this again becomes important when considering how to model what was actually a set of vernacular buildings which, in quite stark contrast to the examples in Aberdeen, had been arranged using an informal overall layout. Indeed, the buildings appeared to have been defined by the shape of the underlying landscape rather than by any order imposed by the architects or master builders at the time. References within the literature to this very subject (Till 2009, referring to comments by Laurie Anderson) drive our attention towards the fact that visual and material complexity in the real world extends quite significantly beyond any notions of our surroundings being somehow defined or flavoured by dirt or imperfection (grit). In the real world, an abstract version of which exists within digital models, we are able to interact with a space, and observe and experience the effects of weather, changing light, the presence and behaviour of other people – in other words, notions of what we might regard as a perfect environment are certainly not frozen in time, and that notion of perfection may in fact emanate from the very complexities which are difficult to represent in a virtual space. Indeed, one of the challenges facing the architectural modeller is that of trying to represent such grit: by coming close to representing reality, we also find ourselves in very real danger of entering the uncanny valley (Mori 1970), where small apparent imperfections in the model may lead to complete perceptual rejection in the mind of the viewer or model user. Where one is intending to deploy such a model in user engagement studies, these dangers become quite significant. Indeed, they could certainly represent a barrier to models and visualisations being accepted as representing a reliable version of what may be likely to emerge once the design and ultimately the construction have been completed.

Digital visualisation in architectural marketing ('true grit')

One aspect of architectural visualisation which became prominent almost as soon as photorealistic digital modelling packages became available was the use of digital models within the marketing of new architecture, and within real estate markets. The use of so-called walk-through videos became common throughout the industry, and with a rapidity which appeared to make it difficult for the industry to pause and reflect upon the impact of such video outputs on client perception, or even on public perception of architecture. It is interesting to consider how the use of architectural visualisation in the marketing of architecture has been enacted, and its likely effect on the perception and subsequent perceived value of architecture – in particular, the extent to which predetermined walk-throughs can be trusted by the viewer, and the importance of being able to control the viewing experience when dealing with digital architecture. It is also interesting to consider the extent to which it is normally possible, or even desirable, to visualise new architecture in a real context and through means which truly capture the complexities of a real physical environment. In that context, we began to explore how 'architecture' can be presented within computer games, where the technological advances towards controllable and even immersive digital environments has arguably been far more rapid than those seen within the architecture and construction industries themselves.

Returning to the study undertaken in the Faeroes, in terms of the architecture itself our model was to a large extent defined by previously undertaken architectural sketches of buildings on the headland, an approximation of the underlying landscape, and by buildings which did not follow any particular or regular plan shape and size. The overall narrowness and undulating topography of the headland at Tinganes (located on the edge of Torshavn) have dictated over time that the buildings take an almost organic approach to village 'layout'. The modern village buildings convey a sense of increasing size and prominence towards the outermost points, with an overall increase in building height, although the use of materials is largely constant throughout. It was felt to be of cultural importance that an assessment and record of such buildings be realised to ensure the site is preserved for the future, and it was felt that the development of an interactive model would help to promote collaborative discussion, debate and greater levels of public participation in the future. For this site, in particular, it was also felt that the proximity of the buildings, and the organic layout of the townscape, meant that appreciation of the site's topography, arrangement and design would be best achieved through navigation and viewing, rather than through the analysis of drawings, plans or photographic stills.

What was also notable about our visit to the Faeroes was that we visited during January, and experienced what is actually quite a rare spell of snowy weather. Coupled with some stormy conditions which had preceded our visit, this presented us with quite a different experience, particularly in comparison to that which one might have during the summer months. For example, many of the timber framed and timber clad buildings in the area had grass covered roofs, some of which had been disturbed by the earlier weather conditions. This meant, ultimately, that

Figure 5.11
Image taken from model of Tinganes, the Faeroes, with comparative site photo (on the left). (Image produced by Stephen Scott.)

Collaboration and participation

Figure 5.12
Image taken from model of Tinganes, the Faeroes, with comparative site photo above. (Image produced by Stephen Scott.)

the digital models we eventually produced as part of the project perhaps have more in common with perfectly maintained examples of the buildings (which might be more prevalent during the warmer months of the year), and I would argue that the project started to raise a number of interesting questions in my own mind regarding the ability of such digital models to accurately represent the 'feeling' of visiting a historic environment. If we think back for a moment to the earlier discussion of the work of Cullen (1961), this extends naturally into considerations of phenomenology, where the emotional and sensual response which one might experience when visiting buildings is very difficult to convey using digital imagery.

While the initial mention of Cullen within this section of the book relates to the experience of moving through that particular townscape, much of the digital modelling work which was undertaken actually concentrated on the translation of the original digital models (produced using 3D Studio) so that they could be run and experienced using an open source games engine (Unreal). We had increasingly begun to feel that games technology, at the time, was moving quite significantly ahead of the software being used to represent architecture from both dynamic and static perspectives. Much of the research did in fact deal with the experience of moving through space, yet we were still representing towns, cities and spaces within our research by using either individual still images, or perhaps a series of still images (following other interesting examples from environmental psychology). Our emerging research hypothesis was that allowing participants in research studies to freely navigate an environment would help us to provide a controlled surrogate environment, which was better suited to reflecting the actual environment under study. Of course, if we were able to take people to every environment we ever wished to study, then this may not be necessary, but the feeling was, given that games technology was increasingly moving online, that this could open up the possibility of allowing participants who would never have the opportunity to visit an actual space to participate in a more immersive form of research.

This aspect of the research brought a number of challenges, which were both technical, in terms of the development of the model, as well as methodological, in terms of the ways that people were able to navigate the virtual space. For the actual modelling process, in the case of this research (which was undertaken in the mid-2000s) the underlying landscape itself, as well as the buildings and even the textures used to represent material on the face of the buildings, were still modelled using a traditional digital modelling process, 3D Studio. The buildings were then converted and reformatted through insertion into a games engine, using a process which was documented by the team at the time (Conniff et al. 2010, Laing et al. 2007). Being able to utilise the model within social science research then became a challenge in itself.

Recording the area involved a measured survey of the site layout and the buildings of significant heritage value. An extensive photographic record of key 'squares' was completed, and an on-site log of important built heritage information was compiled (including such items as building type, construction methods and building materials used). Before modelling of the site could begin, it was important that specific information be gathered relating to the layout and aesthetics of the site. This information took various forms but it is useful if a detailed scale site plan (at least 1:1250) can be obtained, and a detailed photographic study of the site undertaken. It is also useful if basic measurements are physically recorded when visiting the site so they can be referenced back to the site plan to ensure best accuracy.

When photographing the site, it was important to keep in mind that the photographs were to be used as reference material as well as to form the basis for the majority of the textures used within the virtual environment. In the case where buildings are to be photographed, it is preferred that each facade is captured looking straight on to ensure minimal distortion of the image. However, when this is not possible due to immovable obstructions or limited space, Photoshop (or similar image editing software) can be used to adjust the perspective of the photographs.

Previous work in the area of collaborative virtual environments would suggest that networked computers offer the possibility of mediation for human to human interaction, and the opportunity for users to make sense of the information contained within a virtual space (see, for example, Börner 2002). The fact that there has been much research undertaken concerning the manipulation by users of virtual models in real time, for planning and design purposes (Peng et al. 2002a, Peng et al. 2002b), suggests that a dynamic interaction with the processes of heritage assessment should be possible.

Referring back to my comments regarding the use of moving, or user-navigated, digital environments, as opposed to simply presenting respondents with images (which we had typically done in relation to streetscapes and greenspace), the particular research challenge which was set within the study was to explore the effects of user control on the ways in which the users may perceive, remember and understand the environment which they were themselves navigating. In the case of this particular study, the comparison was between walk-throughs of space and the navigation of a similar route where people were able to follow the path using normal games controls (in the case of the study, arrow keys and so on). The main findings from the research were subsequently widely disseminated by the research team (Conniff et al. 2010), and the research raised important issues regarding clarity, and whether people were able to better remember and understand aspects of the scene if they were given control of navigation within the space. One aspect of the research, which we had anticipated encountering, related to the usability of models by people across the respondent group. In particular, a proportion of the respondents experienced feelings akin to motion sickness in both the self-navigated and walk-through portions of the study, as I did myself when observing one of my colleagues navigating the space using one of the large screens in our university. Over the years, I have subsequently had similar experiences using Occulus Rift headsets, typically where I have been presented with a moving scene when my brain is telling me that my body is not actually moving. Producers of both mainstream films and commercially available computer games have long been aware of the potential for this effect, and it is one of the aspects of our own research which does in fact carry significant practical implications for the ways in which digital visualisation is likely to be rolled out and developed in the future (the effect has been reported in the literature, of course, Ohyama et al. 2007).

The other case study which we deal with in this section is more concerned with a consideration of public engagement in the discussion and debate of our built heritage, and how this can be stimulated and enhanced through the use of digital techniques.

Elgin, which is located in the north-east of Scotland, has a documented history of almost 1,000 years. The town as it stands today has

Collaboration and participation

Figure 5.13 **Undertaking laser scanning in Elgin, Scotland. (Photo taken by author.)**

a centre planned around a marketplace and contains a large number of Listed (Scottish legally protected) buildings and monuments. In recent years, a series of projects have been undertaken which included quite extensive laser scanning of aspects of the built heritage in Elgin. The research considered how the technology could be used to record examples of quite small yet significant artefacts or carvings on the faces of walls and buildings, and the process itself caused the research team and participants alike to notice details and examples of the ways in which materials have been used and craftsmen of the area had had a significant effect on the appearance of the town, to an extent which had not been the case during my own early years.[4]

What perhaps struck my colleagues and me most about the process we undertook in Elgin (in a project led by Dr Elizabeth Tait) using laser scanning was not in fact the technical challenge of undertaking the work, or even the research questions concerning how we were likely to use the outputs in the longer term. In the early stages of the work, we undertook to run a series of public events where we demonstrated the laser scanning equipment, but as part of much larger events which were actually about the built heritage of the town. In many cases, there appeared to be as great an interest among audience members in finding out more about the techniques that we were employing, as there was in wishing to discover more about the heritage of the town from the experts and organisers of the meeting. Indeed, at the time we were also utilising mobile-based applications (such as 123D, freely available through Autodesk), which enabled participants to undertake 3D modelling of existing environments, even if they did not have access to expensive equipment such as laser scanners. One began to get the impression that the technology was almost operating as a Trojan horse, in that what were ostensibly discussions about technology and the application of advanced surveying equipment in an unusual set of circumstances did in fact give way to audience members and participants beginning to suggest areas, buildings and artefacts which they felt would benefit from digitisation and recording in a similar manner to that already applied to some formal aspects of the built environment.

Summary

As noted in Chapter 1, it was important in the book to deal with both the technological processes and tools through which collaboration and participation can be fostered and managed, and the theories and practices which might impinge upon the ways in which people collaborate within teams, and the ways and methods through which users and members of the public can be involved in democratic design through participative processes. Following an introductory section which reminded us of some of the underlying theories of participation and collaboration, this chapter served to provide a number of practical examples of how these theories could be brought to bear, or studied in themselves, within applied research. In addition to the descriptions provided of the design and delivery of the visually driven choice-based research, there was the further observation that the studies could only be successful where there was some degree of informed participation from the respondent groups. That is, most of the studies dealt with the consideration of real areas, where the outcomes of the research could in fact have real consequences for the design of those buildings, streets and areas of greenspace.

Returning to the notion of simulation, it was interesting to consider studies undertaken in both Zurich and Aberdeen where issues such as the growth of trees, or the behaviour of individuals (or the possibilities for behaviour) within transport systems, were modelled using a range of software techniques and technologies. These connect with the most recent of the studies described in the chapter, wherein we began to discuss the use of technologies which were able to capture the geometry of an existing environment in high levels of detail. While the majority of the studies described in the chapter focused on themes which are external to the technology itself, much of our own work considering digital heritage has tended to show either that the technology can be used quite effectively as a Trojan Horse, drawing people into the research, or that in some cases it has actually become the focal point of the research in itself.

Notes

1. Our later work concerning greenspace began to see a crossover between architectural and GIS approaches, and in terms of architecture this has arguably now given way to the widespread use of BIM.
2. Aberdeen has developed an award-winning Sustainable Urban Mobility Plan (SUMP), which aims to encourage and support the widespread and accessible use of non-car transport.
3. The prevailing character or atmosphere of a place.
4. I used examples of buildings from Elgin as part of my doctoral studies in the 1990s, and similarly realised that I had failed to 'look up' during the years 1975–1995.

Chapter 6

Future directions

Given the widespread development and application of smart city technology, the need for architecture to embrace the reality and possibilities of data visualisation is likely to emerge as a key driver in future urban design and development. Coupled with the techniques discussed in Chapter 4, this will fundamentally change the way we design, use and live in our built environment. The challenges for visualisation extend well beyond the literal representation of architecture, and begin to embrace visually abstract issues which are both technical and social in nature.

It is useful at this stage to draw together some of the thematic strands which have emerged through the course of the book, and to frame a discussion of future challenges in those terms. We began our discussions of IT in architecture and construction by considering the 'user' of the IT, as well as the user of the architecture (that is, the occupant, owner, people who will be affected by the architecture in their daily lives). Both types of 'user' are essential when attempting to understand how these future relationships between designer, user and technology will change in the coming years.

One could argue that the technology itself (hardware and software) might evolve in the coming years as a result of technical capabilities in themselves leading to developments, but that the technology will be deeply informed by the users (e.g. design teams). One might also argue, to return to our earlier discussion of environmental psychology, that the technology will have a demonstrable effect on the user of the building, but that this relationship between technology and user may be less collaborative than that within the industry, unless efforts are made to ensure that users and occupants of a building, town or city are able to interact with relevant data and information, and in a meaningful manner. Furthermore, whilst the design 'team' will continue to have an effect on the building user, the user(s) themselves will have a growing capacity to impact on the design and the designers. We will discuss these issues of the 'user' in the following sections.

Two other major themes we have addressed in the book were those of **education** and **practice**. From the perspective of collaborative tools, it is useful to consider how their development and application might become prominent and useful within both fields. In the context of education of the design team, a challenge which continues to face the industry is the paradox of cross-discipline collaboration being widely accepted as essential to realising the greatest benefits and avoiding key pitfalls (economic drivers, in particular, are seen in the rationale for BIM adoption put forward by governments and professional bodies, although the success of this will depend on meaningful collaboration), yet this being difficult to enact within education due to separate educational streams and traditions.

Perhaps even more important (given that it is possible with some will to deliver cross-discipline educational project working) is the disconnection between theory and practice of user collaboration and participation, and the place of such activity within the core education of design team professionals. One might argue that an ability to understand the mechanisms (and underlying methodologies) which will lead to effective participation are likely to become core skills in the coming years, and that understanding how this might be affected by technology will form a central and increasingly valuable skill for all designers.

Connected with this is the challenge of integrating deep end-user collaboration and participation within practice, in a manner which does not run the risk of attempting to artificially convert building occupants into designers, or of producing architecture which has been designed by committee.

The speed of change within the digital technology associated within architecture, construction and urban environments has been far more rapid in recent years than that associated with earlier and entirely visual approaches to digitisation. This is due in part to efforts within the industry itself, but has arguably been equally driven and supported through wider changes in society (in that technology and access to information have become pervasive). Whilst early attempts to move technical draughtsmanship from hand drawing towards the use of 2D computer drawing took around 20 or more years to become firmly established (Froese 2013), a move towards data-rich approaches to project definition and representation has taken far less time, and uses technology which is accessible to a wide(r) range of participants.

One example of this is the use of virtual and immersive reality in construction, which has been discussed and researched for many decades.

Future directions

Figure 6.1
Output from laser scan (building interior). (Image created by author.)

While we have been technically able to access the technology necessary to represent architecture using 3D technology for many years, the cost and limited availability have made widespread interactive use of digital models on site difficult. This has been completely revolutionised through the use of cheap tablet devices, with large-scale digital surface interfaces becoming common on (for the meantime) larger construction sites. Laser scanning technology has reduced in price so significantly in the past five years that its use to support conceptual design (through site capture), to record construction as it develops, and to provide a permanent record of buildings and sites, will become pervasive. Likewise, the cost of immersive technology has now reached a low enough price point that its use in computer gaming has certainly overtaken its use as part of professional architecture and engineering.

Nevertheless, what marks these technologies as forming part of a long trajectory which we can trace back to the 1970s is that they emphasise the visual recording and representation of objects in space. Whether we are looking at 2D sketching or 3D modelling, scanning and animation, the emphasis has been on visual representation of what is actually there. A key difference with the technology and software associated with the smart city agenda is that the emphasis moves to consideration of data and information, and how this can be collected, analysed, represented and then made available in a useful manner.

Smart cities and architecture

The opportunity but also the need to recognise the potential for the use of smart technology in our cities, and in our architecture, have emerged

111

in recent years. What has been notable is that in aspects of the constructed environment (perhaps most obviously the transport sector) a consideration of how we use our buildings has meant that there is now an emerging opportunity to make use of ICT, and to do so in a manner which has become pervasive within the early stages of design. This appears to hold the potential to address significant and long recognised issues regarding the use of energy across the constructed environment, and to do so in a manner which reflects wider behaviour and complexities (e.g. behaviour and interrelationships between buildings, services, infrastructure and nature). The emergence of the EU smart cities platform, which evolved into an 'innovation partnership on smart cities and communities', has seen the development of a whole range of activities, including funded research projects and significant efforts to reduce fragmentation between different markets, where markets may well make sense in economic terms but much less sense when we try to consider an integrated open environment. It is interesting to note, among a cluster of aims for the smart cities agenda within Europe, the appearance and centrality of other concerns, including quality of life, competitiveness on industry, and the pursuit of various energy and quiet change targets. In other words, although the technology is in some respects new when considered in such a widespread urban context, the aspirations hark back to long established concerns regarding sustainable development, in a holistic sense (as alluded to in Penn and Al Sayed 2017).

To provide some kind of context, the BSI (2014) emphasise the fact that the world is becoming increasingly urbanised. By 2050, it has been predicted that approximately 80% of the world's population will inhabit cities, and it is likely that the population will still demand the economic and cultural benefits of living in cities, almost despite the consequential demands brought about through increases in population and increasing migration towards urbanisation. The BSI identify smart city technology as one way through which the resources required by cities can be managed, and the suggested definition (BSI 2014) of a smart city is interesting in that it speaks of a collective consideration of physical, digital and human systems. This is important, as it immediately draws us back from the notion of thinking that smart systems, within smart cities, are somehow driven by the digital technology itself. We could reflect back on some of the examples of the research, and some of the case studies, we have touched upon from industry, where we can also recognise that digital technology has typically been applied to help people work together more effectively, or to aid and enhance participation of a wider community in decision making, or simply to make what may appear to be quite complex situations more understandable and transparent to the user. It is also interesting to note that the BSI definition comes with the caveat that any particular city should engage in a 'process of discussion and debates between stakeholders' to define how they may wish to regard the notion of the smart city in their own particular context. The BSI (2014) also went to some considerable lengths to define a number of key concepts, including but not limited to:

- **access rights** (where this aspect of smart cities is intrinsically linked with the wider considerations of open data, and particularly open access to research information). These concepts are connected with wider issues of data ownership and cyber security (including hacking, eavesdropping and confidentiality) and, within the context of creativity and research, related notions of intellectual property rights.
- **software applications** which may be applied
- concepts behind **big data**, where the increasing prevalence of sensor technology to collect information about behaviour and resource use (including energy use, mobility and so on) will require specific consideration of how that data may be stored, and the uses to which it might be put in the future
- **building information modelling** is mentioned at this point in the BSI consideration of smart cities, presumably in the context of how BIM in itself carries great potential across the whole of a life cycle. This is also useful to consider within the context of a smart city as we can begin to understand and appreciate how BIM could ultimately be linked with digital systems which operate outside of systems connected with a single building. Although not within the scope of this book, we can certainly begin to consider some of the implications of smart mobility, where the relationships between housing, places of work, transport routes and autonomous vehicles start to blur demarcation lines and suggested new and innovative uses for data, which have come about through a combination of both technical and behavioural evolution.
- This connects with the concept of the **Internet of things** (IoT), where BSI (2014) describes a situation where objects, environments and vehicles will come to sense and collect large amounts of information, with an associated ability to interact through the Internet, thus becoming a physical extension of what was once a wholly digital system.

Within some of our own current research,[1] we have also encountered real examples of predictive analytics being used to assist with resource management in modern cities, with a particular emphasis on mobility, both personal and the movement of goods and freight.

What is of equal interest, as we think about how digital and smart technology will begin to both shape and support our daily lives in future, is the question of which organisations or which individuals will own and deliver the digital platforms which can be used by all. Returning once more to the concept of user participation and user engagement in the future development of our towns and cities, we need as a society to consider both social and technological implications. From a social perspective, this will include consideration certainly of the open nature of a system, which can be designed in from the outset. This must surely connect, though, with wider socio-economic and environmental concerns, many of which can actually be addressed through the intelligent use of smart data.

For example, the BSI make specific mention of the environmental impact, as well as the environmental potential, of our cities. Some early examples of collective awareness platforms certainly drew on this particular angle of smart cities, by making real-time environmental data available to all citizens, in a manner which attempted to take complex scientific data and make it understandable to the non-expert. From a technical perspective, the subject of digital exclusion and inclusion has become a technically and politically important subject in recent years, with efforts being made by many governments at both national and local level to try to achieve almost 'universal access' to the Internet, perhaps through broadband connectivity.[2] Within our cities, this may be in fact an economically easier challenge to address than in rural areas, simply due to the number of users who may be able to access broadband infrastructure. In a country such as Scotland, where there is great potential to make use of smart technology across the whole of society, this can be hampered where communities are geographically spread, and often in relatively remote rural locations.[3]

Another important concept which appears within the BSI documentation is that of interworking. Given some of our earlier discussions about the long-term use of data, this is likely in itself to become an important and unavoidable topic as time progresses. Whilst the concept itself deals with the notion of data being able to be interconnected across the different types of network, and presumably different types of software, this is likely to be only part of the problem which must be addressed. One could argue in relation to the built environment that the development of BIM has shown one possible way forward with regard to the use of open source, as opposed to proprietary, file formats. This means that information produced within BIM can be easily accessed, read and viewed using open source software. However, this cannot in itself fully counteract the likely effects of varying data types, and even methods to access that data, changing or becoming redundant over time. Therefore, the subject of interworking or interoperability between systems is one which will almost inevitably require continuous monitoring throughout the life cycle not only of individual buildings but also of a townscape as a whole.

The BSI make reference (BSI Standards Publication PAS 181:2014) to UK government challenges driving change for cities in the UK:

- economic restructuring
- urban infrastructure (particularly in relation to housing and transport)
- climate change
- retail provision, and the changing nature of high streets
- adult social care
- local authority budgets.

One can observe that these challenges relate to both the availability of resources to a town or city, and the ability of those towns and cities to be resilient in the face of a changing external environment. Whilst those external pressures might be economic, environmental or driven by social change, it is the 'complexity and pace of change' (BSI Standards Publication 2014) which demands an integrated response, and one which extends across departments, sectors and arguably well beyond the concept of the public and private sector. In developing a framework to assist in the formulation and delivery of smart cities, it is interesting to note, particularly in the light of our earlier discussions concerning participation and engagement of citizens, that the areas which have been identified as requiring enabling include:

- shifting the emphasis for driving change with regard to city spaces and systems towards **current** and **future citizens**. What is again notable from the BSI guidance is the correlation between having an emphasis on the role of citizens in the design and delivery of services within city, and the development of digital systems which are accessible, ubiquitous and founded on the notion of openness and sharing of data.
- integration of **physical** and **digital planning** (which in itself may in fact begin to increase accessibility of the planning system to a wider range of participants)
- helping cities to **respond** to challenges in a **systematic** and **agile** manner.

The guidance is also quite clear when it comes to the idea of developing a city vision, and this connects directly back to our earlier discussions of collaboration among citizens, collaboration among 'formal' decision makers and those citizens, and support for what is described as the development of a city vision through a process of iteration and collaboration. This connects with wider current thinking within theories of urban design, where some of the notions of top-down decision making have indeed started to give way to the use of not only digital but also social systems to support urban interventions which are in themselves responsive to change, reflective of the inherent complexity with urban systems, and which require a cycle of intervention followed by reflection, monitoring and adjustment (Miguel, Laing and Zaman 2016).

The BSI reflect this (BSI Standards Publication 2014) to some extent through the suggestion that stakeholder engagement programmes should be established and led by a senior executive within any given city. Bearing in mind our earlier discussions of what might in fact be referred to when we consider the notions of collaboration and participation, it goes without saying that the use of an expansive and pervasive open data platform should indeed be flexible and adaptable, and open to new forms of collaboration and participation as engagement in a system evolves, and as the technical capabilities of systems change over time. In seeking to establish a decision-making framework which can operate effectively within the smart city of the future, there is indeed a need to find mechanisms which support city data being shared across platforms, and in a manner which is interoperable between those systems and between different types of user (BSI Standards Publication 2017). Bearing this in mind, we can draw on that same guidance to consider how the data contained within systems, and within digital models, will inevitably invite categorisation. These categories are interesting in themselves, in that they hold significant resonance with the ways in which we may consider the use of data within BIM, which again suggests that the efforts being made to ensure the standardised use of data within BIM will in the fullness of time enable building information models initially created for the purposes of supporting design, construction and delivery of individual buildings to be integrated within a much wider city data platform:

- **Infrastructure** refers mainly to the infrastructure required to operate a city.
- **Metadata** could refer to participants, organisations or other such contextual information which can be connected with data collected and stored within a system. We refer elsewhere to work concerning the implementation of sustainable transport systems within cities, where examples of meta data might include the users of any particular system and user behaviour (travel mode).

- **Reference** data might refer to specific information regarding building energy systems, or even vehicle specification data (for example types of fuel, efficiency, age, and so on), thus drawing overt connections within the complex system of buildings, infrastructure, mobility options and so on.
- **Thematic** data could refer to the services which are provided by a local authority, and required by most or even all of the citizens of a city (energy, waste management, communications, transport, health, housing and so on).

Documentation and the definition of terms which relate to smart cities also deal with the notions of civic engagement and governance processes. In relation to civic engagement in particular, it is interesting to note that the documentation itself (PAS 181, BSI Standards Publication 2014) states that whilst smart city applications hold the capacity to enhance civic engagement, there is always a risk that the same applications could potentially disenfranchise communities, through issues of technical accessibility. It needs to be ensured that systems are built around user needs, rather than around city organisational structures (page 8), with the possibility of citizens being able to significantly influence decision making within their own town or city.

This aspect of architecture and the emerging connections between architecture and data-rich technologies (including sensors) are likely to connect in the coming years with many of the issues discussed in the preceding section. What is important about the notion of thinking of new architecture in the context of the wider environment is that it causes us to think quite significantly beyond the idea that participation in architecture is limited to those involved in design construction and even the use of a specific building. There will be an increasing need for a new architecture, and to some extent existing buildings which have been retrofitted, to be able to provide accurate and real-time information regarding a building's collective energy and resource use, and how it is connected with other buildings and facilities in any given town or city. When one refers to a much wider range of individuals and groups being affected by such architecture, this reminds us of methods and ways through which people could derive 'value' from an object or good, and this could extend to people who may not come into direct contact with, or have the specific need to use, an object, service, facility or building (one could refer more widely to a long history of research within environmental economics, where such values have been derived both through observation of actual markets and the expressed preferences and values of individuals). In the case of my own early studies, which tended to deal with examples

Future directions

Figure 6.2
Photographs reflecting the visual complexity of an urban route (in this case, a walk to school).
(All four photos taken by author.)

Future directions

from the historic built environment, examples of value which can be derived from a building (even if it were not being used by the participant) would tend to reside within consideration of how that building might be regarded as something that should be passed on to future generations (in an almost altruistic manner), with clear evidence of people valuing buildings and objects simply because they knew they existed. This might relate to more prominent examples of the built environment (for example buildings which are regarded as holding significant national or cultural value) or to smaller-scale objects or monuments which hold particular memories or emotional values for any given person. This also relates to the pedestrian ways and networks suggested by Cullen (1961), which create a 'human town' which must in itself be a connected whole (to match the vehicular network).

Within the context of smart cities, our consideration of value is slightly different. That is, we may wish to think more deeply about the provision of data, and useful methods to access that data, as holding value for an individual even where they have no particular need to interact with that data at the moment. We are, of course, already able to interact with cities using versions of augmented reality, and this has been the case for a number of years. Typically using GPS to locate the use of a mobile application within any particular environment, it became possible to generate a real-time feedback regarding the position of particular facilities, for example restaurants, transport hubs and so on. What is likely to differentiate the smart city from this set of circumstances is that feedback will be more connected with sensor technology located within the buildings themselves. This will enable information to be updated in real time, and will significantly widen the usefulness of such data. Within architecture and construction, and as we have discussed to some extent in preceding sections dealing with BIM and facilities management, pervasive technology which is likely to become the norm in coming years will mean that building components are able to self-diagnose issues as they emerge, and will become capable of alerting the estates manager.

This train of thought, however, should not blind us to the fact that such pervasive technology is likely to radically alter the ways in which we design and subsequently use architecture. Therefore, considerations of how technology can be employed to improve or augment existing processes and tasks (such as recording of building maintenance tasks) potentially miss the more fundamental changes which will happen in the coming years. The impact of smart technology, including the use of sensor technology to monitor resource use, behaviour and connections between the two, will have a deep effect on how we design new architecture.

Particularly when we bear in mind the aspirations of the smart city, where buildings and the surrounding urban environment are augmented through the use of ICT, we also open the possibility of seriously considering the use of crowd sourced data. This connects most importantly with the notion of a smart city in the sense that we are able to then engage with the potential of real-time feedback. The reality of enabling the users of cities and buildings to provide feedback in terms of their performance (perhaps energy use, heating, levels of comfort or mobility patterns) is such that participation then becomes something that extends well beyond the design phase.

With particular regard to applications which might be applied within the built environment, we are already seeing specific applications being offered in relation to individual sectors, which in turn refer back to some of the priority areas identified at the European level. These include the use of real-time feedback with regard to mobility and the use of mass public transit within cities, but also moves towards citizens being able to take control of personal mobility in ways which were not previously possible. Although at the current time the most obvious manifestation of this may well be on-demand personal transport systems, these are still typically limited to systems which in many respects only differ from corporate modes of transport in terms of the private or individual ownership and use of vehicles. In the future it is far more likely that we will see the use of autonomous vehicles (in terms of technical development), whilst it is also extremely likely that the desire on the part of cities, or on the part of municipal decision makers, to offer significant support for the use of shared mobility (for example, car sharing as opposed to mass transit) could be readily assisted by the combined use of mobile devices and distributed information systems.

Representation though collaborative devices

It is also useful to consider at this stage the use of both immersive and augmented reality within construction. This has in itself been a focus of much academic research in recent years, and an area of study which started to see applications being rolled out on-site. Again referring to some earlier discussions in the text where we consider architecture from the perspective of the whole life cycle, we must also consider how the use of immersive augmented reality could be helpful across that same life cycle. This has certainly been reflected in academic research, which has tended to focus on immersive reality during the construction (and even earlier design) stages, but which in more recent years has started to consider how augmented reality in particular could be useful to the facilities manager when attempting to understand and catalogue the implications of building maintenance decisions in the much longer term.

Gaming

In earlier chapters, we also touched upon the notion of gaming technology being of particular use within the representation of architectural design. In the research with which I have been personally involved, the main benefit of engaging with gaming technology was to allow the users of digital models to freely navigate virtual space themselves. Much of my own earlier research had in fact used fully populated digital models, where we placed great emphasis on the representation of 'real' spaces within the models, and this provided some kind of digital surrogate. Nevertheless, we were also well aware of the inherent difficulties in undertaking such modelling, including the problems associated with representing non-visual information. This extended beyond the problems we might have encountered when trying to represent different environmental conditions (as referred to in Aspinall et al. 2010, for example), and instead focused on our desire to allow the research participants to have some kind of self-directed and interactive experience when experiencing digital architecture.

What perhaps marked out that research experience as being different from what is likely to happen in the future was the probability that many of the research participants were neither used to the experience of working with 3D computer games or models, nor likely to have had any experience of building and designing games or digital models themselves. In the coming years, this will simply no longer be the case. The popularity among younger computer users of games such as *Minecraft*, where the emphasis is actually on the construction of digital models, means that the novelty of interacting with 3D digital spaces will no longer carry in itself the same elements of surprise as they did in the past. This represents an opportunity for both research and practice, in the sense that asking users of buildings, or participants in the design process, to interact with digital virtual space will be unlikely to place any kind of technical barrier between the participant and the technology. The uses for this could potentially exist and be realised at any stage of the design and subsequent building use phases. To refer back to some of our earlier discussion, the potential uses within both facilities management (for individual buildings), and in relation to the engagement of citizens when actively discussing the future of our urban areas and towns, carry the greatest interest within the context of this book.

Building information modelling, as we have discussed, has clear potential for incorporation and development as a core part of the conceptual and technical design stages. If we think about the Bew and Richards model, we can also begin to see the potential for BIM to have a significant and positive effect on the longer life cycle. Indeed, within the construction industry in recent years there has been an interest in and emphasis on the application of BIM, but this has tended to focus on the technical design and construction phases. There are good reasons for this, including:

- the need within most BIM software packages to include information about material and technical detail (thus forming a potential step away from wider conceptual design – for discussion and debate!)
- a recognition that BIM digital models lend themselves to assisting the delivery phase (e.g. construction and supply chains), and
- the fact that there still remains a strong connection between client, construction, design and delivery teams up to the end of the construction phase.

Although various government agendas globally (including 'soft landings' in the UK) have stressed the need to aim for continuity and ongoing responsibilities once into the operational phase, there remains the fact that all parties (including the client) might change once a building is occupied. Therefore, whilst many practitioners and researchers would argue that taking a longer-term 'cradle to grave' view of architecture should be useful in almost all contexts, the reality in practice is that this remains a challenge (including a potential disconnection between the choices and players which 'cause' cost and value and those who will feel the 'effects').

One of the obvious benefits which can be derived from BIM, if applied as a 'live' model at the construction phase, is that the model at the point of handover (as discussed with respect to soft landings) should be fit for purpose as a model/document which can remain 'live' during the following years. One could also argue that the usefulness of *any* digital file becomes precarious as time progresses, and particularly if not regularly in use, due to the dangers of data or format obsolescence. On the other hand, a BIM which is updated to note and monitor the natural evolution of a building over time should hold huge potential value to the facilities manager, client and building user.

As we move towards a situation where BIM has become pervasive, we can foresee over a short period of time that the emphasis on BIM within larger new-build projects will decrease. In fact, it was interesting to note that one of the first RICS ventures into BIM as an organisation was the digital recording (scanning) of their existing HQ in London. From this, one wonders if we can begin to see a picture emerging where the benefits of having a BIM *per se* extend far beyond that of the early 'work stages'. One important point highlighted by Pickford (2015) is that BIM by its very nature places an emphasis on post-occupancy evaluation (POE). That the software is capable of prediction and simulation of building performance at the deign stage invites the collection and monitoring of actual performance once construction is complete. The potential for such POE to feed back into future new builds and new design also suggests a natural extension of the role of the facilities manager. Having said this, the current provisions of data structures and data drops in mainstream BIM guidance, mandates and protocols lack some of the detail which may be required by the facilities manager in practice.

With particular reference to the emerging use of BIM within facilities management, there does appear to be a disconnection between the technical capabilities of a system and the extent to which it is actually being used by estates managers (Eadie et al. 2013). Despite the ease with which the construction team, including the design team, could provide a final data drop (Cobie dataset) and hand over a fully populated 3D model of the building to a client, this was in fact not happening in over 70% of the projects studied. Interestingly, the ability within such information-rich models to produce visualisations of what the building might look like was thought to be less significant by respondents to that study than issues of collaboration, management, reduction of waste and accuracy of information. Also of note is that the study appeared to indicate investments in training and re-education as being not so significant that smaller practices were unable to engage. Of course, we must bear in mind that we may in fact be looking at responses from those who have chosen to engage in the implementation of a particular process, as opposed to responses from a more widely representative industry sample. Whether early adoption gives way to mass adoption will be interesting to trace in the coming years.

Eadie and colleagues (2013) also noted, correctly, that the relatively recent adoption of BIM as a new approach to digital modelling at the technical design and construction stages means that it is difficult to give a definitive assessment as to how the technology is likely to continue to be embraced during the much longer life cycle of the building. Nevertheless, one would have to intuitively presume that, where the use of BIM as an estates management tool has not been planned for the design stage, the likelihood of subsequent adoption would appear to be quite slight.

Just as the industry during the 1990s expended considerable effort discussing the frequent absence of the builder at the design stage as being a significant problem in terms of being able to address issues of buildability, one could also argue that the absence of a facilities manager as a BIM is being developed would significantly reduce the chances of the resulting models being used during the life cycle. Elsewhere, Isikdag and Underwood (2010) drew our attention to the need for different types of model at each stage of a building's life cycle. Although each version of the model would contain broadly similar data, we nevertheless never deviate, at a theoretical level, from the notion that BIMs can act as 'the shared information backbone through the life cycle of the project'. Where we arguably need to be careful is in presuming that the technical ability for BIMs to provide such a tool for use throughout the life cycle is likely to be enacted. It is perhaps notable also that some of the more prominent examples and case studies of BIM in practice have tended to relate to very large-scale projects.

I spoke in Chapter 5 of research concerning image manipulation, and the ways in which this could be used within what were actually user consultation studies. In the wider context of those research projects, one important aspect which tended to flavour the responses obtained, and the extent to which people were willing to participate in research, related back to the ownership of buildings, and the ownership of architecture. That is, where we are dealing with very large-scale projects (such as hospitals, university buildings and buildings which are constructed for and used by the public sector) there will in most instances be some consistency between the team which is involved at the design and construction phases and at least some members of the team who will be involved during the rest of the life cycle. Even in the case of projects which have been constructed using mechanisms such as the private finance initiative (PFI), there will still be (perhaps even more so) some objective reason at the design stage to find this continuity across the whole of the life cycle. That this has not happened in the case of some projects is perhaps more down to managerial failure, rather than being an intrinsic or inevitable part of the process. In the case of my own research concerning the built heritage, this continuity was simply not in place. This meant that the individuals, or the organisations, who were involved in making interventions in historic buildings (for example cleaning of the stonework or replacement of windows and doors) were very often doing so primarily for the reason that it would make the building more marketable. This meant that there was a break during the life cycle in terms of ownership, and consequently that there was also, arguably, a break in terms of perceived responsibility for the building. By extension, and in the case of information-rich digital modelling (BIM), whilst one can see strong reasons for this being implemented through the design and construction phases, there will often be instances of buildings where even things like ownership of the as-built model will not be clear, and where there is likely to be little or no continuity in terms of the participants involved.

One should also bear in mind that digital data, perhaps much more than paper-based architectural designs, actually holds another significant risk, that of being lost through time through changes in storage media or even in the security of that data storage. Should a facilities manager choose to re-engage with the as-built BIM five years after handover, who is to say whether the files will still remain readable, or if the files will even be stored on media which is still accessible?[4]

When one considers the application of facilities management within the built environment, it is often regarded as being a stage which will become operational once a building has been handed over to a client. Whilst this may continue to be the case in practical terms, initiatives such as that of 'soft landings' (www.bimtaskgroup.org/gsl/) have begun to blur the distinction between delivery and operation, and the ethos of BIM has tended to move us towards regarding the life cycle as being central to the design process, and to the whole of the plan of work. For those of us who have been active in terms of life cycle assessment and life cycle costing for many years, such concepts are not new, and it has been accepted for decades that the financial cost (and value) of built assets during the operational phase far outstrips that of the initial design and construction (www.wbdg.org/resources/lcca.php).

Citizen engagement

Some early examples of visualisation which we have described in this book, and indeed some examples which I have used within my own research (including those looking at streetscapes), tend to fall into the category of projects where the aim was to represent what something was going to look like, should some change or intervention be enacted. However, other projects and case studies which we have considered, including those looking at greenspace and increasingly those which are regarded as heritage projects, have placed certainly as much emphasis on the information underpinning those models, and information which then emerges once people begin to discuss the models, as they have on the aesthetic appearance of the visualisations themselves. As the construction industry has moved towards a paradigm for modelling which is based around simulation, within which the appearance of models has remained vital, I would argue that the centrality of information and data visualisation for construction and architecture is likely to become increasingly important and prominent.

To return to our earlier discussion of the importance of drawing, sketching and the aesthetic value of architecture, we must not lose sight of the fact that such underlying information and data should be recorded, and it should be provided in the service of a wider design task, and in the longer term in the service of building performance, to ensure that buildings meet the needs of their users and occupants. Extending this thread further, we should then consider who the users of these models are likely to be. Where the users are in fact site operatives, engaged in the initial construction process itself, providing models which go significantly beyond showing what a building is ultimately going to look like, and which perhaps have augmented characteristics in comparison to traditional construction drawings, is likely to be of greatest use. That is, somebody responsible for the construction of the steel frame may take some value from knowing how that frame will in the longer term sit within the final construction, but will ultimately wish to know how the frame is to be erected, jointed and finished. This argument could extend to any of the trades existing on-site. The case of the estates manager or the facilities manager is perhaps slightly different, in that some knowledge of the aesthetic effects of any choices may in fact be quite useful. For example, an ability to 'look' at the current environment, as it is in place at the moment, with the capability of using augmented reality to 'see' how the choice of a range of finishes will affect the aesthetic appearance of a space could be genuinely useful. Being able to overlay on top of this visual information the likely effects of various alternatives on cost, maintenance schedules or even the energy which will be used by the building would add considerably to the usefulness of the data models and could significantly improve the value of the work undertaken by that individual.

Summary

This chapter draws together some of the key strands within the book, most notably those of the building user and the groups and individuals who might 'participate' in the design, and the manner in which this may be facilitated by the advent of smart cities. This is likely to go hand-in-hand with an increasingly pervasive use of IT within the architecture and construction industry, and although the emphasis and many current examples in this book and industry relate to 'building information modelling', this is very likely to become part of a wider digital landscape in the coming years.

Many of the public participation examples we considered in earlier chapters might be regarded as activities and projects which emerged from a combination of willing parties and local policy. These tended to make use of IT, visualisation and engagement tools in ways which suited a particular activity (e.g. online engagement or the presentation of design scenarios). Through such work, though, it has been possible to demonstrate how such activities can be effective, and the incorporation of aspects of the 'ladder of participation' in digitally supported collective awareness platforms will form a key strand of the emerging smart city. Likewise, the usefulness of BIM will begin to extend beyond individual construction projects, whereby buildings in use are able to both make use of and contribute to wider data platforms and wider data environments.

Many of the technologies discussed and described in the book (most notably, perhaps, laser scanning and photogrammetry) have moved from being niche to market-wide and widely accessible (in terms of both usability and price). Therefore, the opportunity for communities to engage through the production of digital data will be only likely to increase in the coming years.

Notes

1. For example, Civitas PORTIS (http://civitas.eu/portis, accessed 24 April 2018) explores the use of smart data to provide real-time feedback with regard to urban mobility.
2. For example, we can read of initiatives in the Highlands and Islands of Scotland: www.hie.co.uk/community-support/community-broadband-scotland/ (accessed 24 April 2018).
3. The importance of connecting rural communities has been long recognised as an enabler for social and economic reasons, as within the Scottish Highlands and Islands (www.hie.co.uk/regional-information/digital-highlands-and-islands/, accessed 24 April 2018).
4. The sorry tale of numerous now-obsolete data storage devices and technologies has been recounted elsewhere, not least in relation to the storage of video (www.obsoletemedia.org/laserdisc/, accessed 24 April 2018).

Chapter 7

Final remarks

This book concerns the connected subjects and practices of collaboration and participation in architectural design. Due in no small part to the manner in which digital tools and techniques are having an effect on the architecture and construction industry, part of the discussion has inevitably dealt with collaboration within the design team itself. What is of particular interest at the moment, and perhaps signals the industry being at something of a crossroads, is the emphasis on digital tools and techniques which appear to facilitate a collaboration of sorts – sharing of data, sharing of information and the ability for teams consisting of multiple disciplines to work together, even when physically at a distance from one another.

I suggest that this signals a crossroads for the industry as the challenge of collaboration remains exactly that, a challenge which must be addressed. As I have noted elsewhere in the text, the extent of this challenge is exemplified by the long time period over which the industry has in fact ruminated on the potential benefits, yet also the genuine barriers, involved in the need to encourage participants from different disciplines to work closely together. The emerging digital technology to help assist with that process is without a doubt of significant benefit and use within the industry, but we cannot deny the real problems which exist in terms of behaviour, cross-discipline education and even the need to have shared goals across an entire team. In order to realise deeper and more meaningful collaboration within practice, the solution to these problems extends well beyond the provision of digital tools.

Nevertheless, significant developments in both software (most notably, arguably, in the field of building information modelling) and hardware (for example data capture, as well as team collaboration tools, including augmented reality devices) have meant that the possibility of collaboration has become more real, with an associated ability across the whole of the industry to realise some of the aspirations of the 1970s. This includes

Final remarks

the integrated use of sketching within digital working, which has often been advocated and demonstrated to be incredibly effective as a method to capture information about the development of design, including the iterative development of new ideas. Making use of the ability within data-rich digital models to contain such information holds real potential, and will be likely to significantly shape the manner in which we design in teams for years to come. As we also deal with in the book, though, challenges still exist with regard to the development of digital tools which can be regarded as helpful and are supportive of the design process, even at the conceptual stages. It is within this realm that we may see the greatest advances of software technology, particularly in that specifically used by the design team, in the coming years.

A remarkable feature which can be observed in the adoption of BIM (to date) has been the willingness of the industry as a whole to engage with information-rich 3D models. Although the argument has often been made that BIM is not about software, and that the intentions behind any drivers to adopt BIM are not technologically or software driven, we cannot avoid the technological imperative that is connected with digital modelling in a way that is fundamentally different from working practice up until now. A major and most obvious deviation from historical practice, regarding the modelling workflow within BIM, is that models are

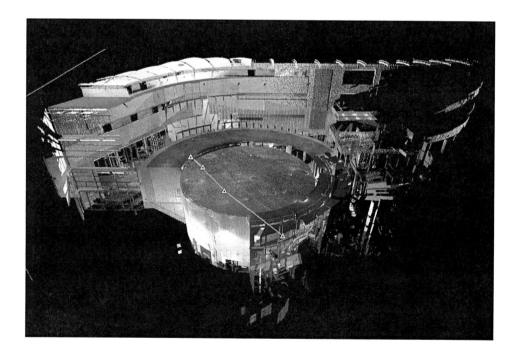

Figure 7.1
Output from laser scan (building interior). (Image created by author.)

constructed from an information base rather than from considerations of aesthetics, spatial layout or other visual aspirations. Although it is obviously still vitally important that any architectural designs emerging from a building information modelling environment meet these aspirations, one must begin to regard any models which emerge from BIM as a precursor to or potential surrogate for buildings which *will actually be constructed*. Therefore, a challenge remains for the digital modelling environment to support the use of BIM software at the conceptual design stage.

A further issue that would be useful for us to discuss as we close is that of data acquisition. For understandable reasons, much of the emphasis within building information modelling in the past few years has been placed on new designs and new construction. However, within many parts of the world (and within Europe this is a particularly pressing matter) it is the case that most of the buildings which will exist in 2025 have already been constructed. In order that we can derive greatest benefit from the 'nD' capabilities of building information modelling, including environmental analysis, health and safety assessment, facilities management and suchlike, there will be an increasing need to ensure that buildings constructed some time ago have suitably information-rich building information models prepared. In recent years, there has been a reasonable amount of effort devoted to the collection of such geometric data, often making use of emerging advanced technologies including terrestrial laser scanning and photogrammetry.

As we move into an era where the use and application of BIM and associated digital tools become the norm, there will be an increasing expectation that 'dimensions' of data beyond the geometric will become ever more valuable:

- 4D – time (to capture process and evolution)
- 5D – schedule and cost
- 6D – life cycle management.

As level 2 BIM becomes more widely adopted, within both the public and private sectors, it is likely that the future of BIM will become increasingly driven by benefits and opportunities which emerge from practice, as well as from the raft of government and academically driven research currently ongoing. Whether the whole design process and life cycle (including conceptual design and the treatment of existing buildings) will be embraced within that evolution remains to be seen. Nevertheless, it seems inevitable that the potential for a much deeper use of the data contained within building information models will rapidly be realised within mainstream practice.

With regard to the participation of the end users of architecture, what is interesting from the work surveyed and illustrated within this book is the manner in which such participative work can extend theories and practices which were established long before the visualisation tools which are now commonly used within both research and practice. It is particularly interesting, in particular, to return to the theoretical ladder of participation, as this helps us to place methods, practice and digital tools within some kind of theoretical framework. Whilst there is certainly an established and quite long practice within our industry of using 3D digital visualisation in the marketing of architecture, for property development or real estate purposes, one might argue that the use of technology in such a manner does not in fact help us reach much higher than the first rung (Arnstein 1969). Throughout our discussions, we have also touched upon notions of the realism of such architectural visualisations, and some of the problems which can in fact arise where even small aspects of the images used appear to be unrealistic or draw attention away from the intended focus of an image. Of more importance to the central concerns of this book, where we wish to explore how the genuine participation of end users and wider community groups might take place within architectural design, are the ways in which we can actually arrive at meaningful *participation*, as opposed to simple consultation of the people who are expected to *receive* architecture. In this sense, we inevitably return to the consideration of how technologies may be used to facilitate engagement, or how technologies can be used to facilitate meaningful and useful dialogue between designers and end users.

References

Al-kheder, S., Al-shawabkeh, Y. & Haala, N. 2009, 'Developing a documentation system for desert palaces in Jordan using 3D laser scanning and digital photogrammetry', *Journal of Archaeological Science*, vol. 36, no. 2, pp. 537–546.

Andrew, C., Young, M. & Tonge, K. 1994, *Stone cleaning: a guide for practitioners*, Historic Scotland, Edinburgh.

Aouad, G., Lee, A. & Wu, S. 2005, 'From 3D to nD modelling', *ITcon*, vol. 10, pp. 15–16.

Appleyard, D. 1976, 'Understanding professional media – issues, theory, and a research agenda', in *Human behaviour and environment: advances in theory and research*, eds. I. Altman & J. Wohlwill, Plenum Press, New York, pp. 43–88.

Arniani, M., Badii, A., De Liddo, A., Georgi, S., Passani, A., Piccolo, L.S.G. & Teli, M. 2014, *Collective awareness platforms for sustainability and social innovation: an introduction*, Creative Commons, http://booksprints-for-ict-research.eu/wp-content/uploads/2014/07/BS5-CAPS-FIN-003.pdf, accessed 24 April 2018.

Arnstein, S.R. 1969, 'A ladder of citizen participation', *Journal of the American Institute of Planners*, vol. 35, no. 4, pp. 216–224.

Aspinall, P.A., Thompson, C.W., Alves, S., Sugiyama, T., Brice, R. & Vickers, A. 2010, 'Preference and relative importance for environmental attributes of neighbourhood open space in older people', *Environment and Planning B: Planning and Design*, vol. 37, no. 6, pp. 1022–1039.

Balletti, C., Ballarin, M. & Guerra, F. 2017, '3D printing: state of the art and future perspectives', *Journal of Cultural Heritage*, vol. 26, pp. 172–182.

Bar-Eli, S. 2013, 'Sketching profiles: awareness to individual differences in sketching as a means of enhancing design solution development', *Design Studies*, vol. 34, no. 4, pp. 472–493.

References

Belardi, P. 2014, *Why architects still draw*, Massachusetts Institute of Technology, Cambridge, MA.

Bilda, Z. & Demirkan, H. 2003, 'An insight on designers' sketching activities in traditional versus digital media', *Design Studies*, vol. 24, no. 1, pp. 27–50.

Bilda, Z., Gero, J.S. & Purcell, T. 2006, 'To sketch or not to sketch? That is the question', *Design Studies*, vol. 27, no. 5, pp. 587–613.

Bishop, I.D., Wherrett, J.R. & Miller, D.R. 2001, 'Assessment of path choices on a country walk using a virtual environment', *Landscape and Urban Planning*, vol. 52, no. 4, pp. 225–237.

Börner, K. 2002, 'Twin worlds: augmenting, evaluating, and studying three-dimensional digital cities and their evolving communities', in *Digital cities II: computational and sociological approaches*, eds. M. Tanabe, P. van den Besselaar and T. Ishida, Springer-Verlag, Berlin, pp. 256–269.

Broadbent, G. 1988, *Design in architecture: architecture and the human senses*, revised reprint edn, David Fulton Publishers, London.

BSI Standards Publication 2014, *PAS 180:2014 Smart cities – vocabulary*, British Standards Institution, London.

BSI Standards Publication 2014, *PAS 181:2014 Smart city framework: guide customer service to establishing strategies for smart cities and communities*, British Standards Institution, London.

BSI Standards Publication 2017, *PAS 183:2017 Smart cities: guide to establishing a decision-making framework for sharing data and information services*, British Standards Institution, London.

Bustillo, A., Alaguero, M., Miguel, I., Saiz, J.M. & Iglesias, L.S. 2015, 'A flexible platform for the creation of 3D semi-immersive environments to teach Cultural Heritage', *Digital Applications in Archaeology and Cultural Heritage*, vol. 2, no. 4, pp. 248–259.

Carver, S. 2003, 'The future of participatory approaches using geographic information: developing a research agenda for the 21st century', *Journal of the Urban and Regional Information Systems Association*, vol. 15, no. APA I, pp. 61–71.

Chen, C. 2005, 'Top 10 unsolved information visualization problems', *IEEE Computer Graphics and Applications*, vol. 25, no. 4, pp. 12–16.

Conniff, A., Craig, T., Laing, R. & Galán-Díaz, C. 2010, 'A comparison of active navigation and passive observation of desktop models of future built environments', *Design Studies*, vol. 31, no. 5, pp. 419–438.

Coyne, R., Park, H. & Wiszniewski, D. 2002, 'Design devices: digital drawing and the pursuit of difference', *Design Studies*, vol. 23, no. 3, pp. 263–286.

Cullen, G. 1961, *The Concise Townscape*, Architectural Press, New York.

Davies, A. 2004, *Using images to present stated preference information: an application to the built environment*, PhD thesis, Robert Gordon University.

Davies Cooper, R.F. & Cooper, C.L. 1984, 'Effect of new technology on the work and methods of the typographic designer', *Design Studies*, vol. 5, no. 1, pp. 21–29.

Demirkan, H. 2005, 'Generating design activities through sketches in multi-agent systems', *Automation in Construction*, vol. 14, no. 6, pp. 699–706.

Dossick, C.S. & Neff, G. 2011, 'Messy talk and clean technology: communication, problem-solving and collaboration using building information modelling', *Engineering Project Organization Journal*, vol. 1, no. 2, pp. 83–93.

Eadie, R., Browne, M., Odeyinka, H., McKeown, C. & McNiff, S. 2013, 'BIM implementation throughout the UK construction project lifecycle: an analysis', *Automation in Construction*, vol. 36, pp. 145–151.

Eastman, C.M. 1974, 'Through the looking glass: why no wonderland? Computer applications to architecture in the USA', *Computer Aided Design*, vol. 6, no. 3, pp. 119–124.

Egan, J. 1998, *Rethinking construction: the report of the construction task force*, Department of Trade and Industry, London.

Eris, O., Martelaro, N. & Badke-Schaub, P. 2014, 'A comparative analysis of multimodal communication during design sketching in co-located and distributed environments', *Design Studies*, vol. 35, no. 6, pp. 559–592.

Fonseca, D., Valls, F., Redondo, E. & Villagrasa, S. 2016, 'Informal interactions in 3D education: citizenship participation and assessment of virtual urban proposals', *Computers in Human Behavior*, vol. 55, Part A, pp. 504–518.

Froese, T. 2013, 'Trends in information and communication technologies for construction: past, present and future', *Proceedings of the 2013 IEEE 17th International Conference on Computer Supported Cooperative Work in Design (CSCWD) IV*, eds. Weiming Shen, Weidong Li, Jean-Paul Barthès, Junzhou Luo, Haibin Zhu, Jianming Yong & Xiaoping Li, Springer-Verlag, Berlin, p. 2.

Hakonen, A., Kuusela, J. & Okkonen, J. 2015, 'Assessing the application of laser scanning and 3D inspection in the study of prehistoric cairn sites: the case study of Tahkokangas, northern Finland', *Journal of Archaeological Science: Reports*, vol. 2, pp. 227–234.

Harrington, B. & O'Connell, M. 2016, 'Video games as virtual teachers: prosocial video game use by children and adolescents from different socioeconomic groups is associated with increased empathy and prosocial behaviour', *Computers in Human Behavior*, vol. 63, pp. 650–658.

Heft, H. & Nasar, J. 2000, 'Evaluating environmental scenes using dynamic versus static displays', *Environment and Behaviour*, vol. 32, pp. 301–322.

Held, R.T., Cooper, E.A., O'Brien, J.F. & Banks, M.S. 2010, 'Using blur to affect perceived distance and size', *ACM Transactions on Graphics*, vol. 29, no. 2, p. 19.

Hornsby, S. 1992, 'Patterns of Scottish emigration to Canada, 1750–1870', *Journal of Historical Geography*, vol. 18, no. 4, pp. 397–416.

Hunter, A.J.S., Steiniger, S., Sandalack, B.A., Liang, S.H.L., Kattan, L., Shalaby, A.S., Alaniz Uribe, F., Bliss-Taylor, C.A.M. & Martinson, R. 2012, 'PlanYourPlace.ca – a geospatial infrastructure for sustainable community planning', *Revue Internationale de Géomatique*, vol. 22, no. 2, pp. 223–253.

Hyde, R. 1989, 'Design procedures in architectural design: applications in CAAD', *Design Studies*, vol. 10, no. 4, pp. 239–245.

Ibrahim, R. & Pour Rahimian, F. 2010, 'Comparison of CAD and manual sketching tools for teaching architectural design', *Automation in Construction*, vol. 19, no. 8, pp. 978–987.

Isikdag, U. & Underwood, J. 2010, 'Two design patterns for facilitating building information model-based synchronous collaboration', *Automation in Construction*, vol. 19, no. 5, pp. 544–553.

Israel, J.H., Wiese, E., Mateescu, M., Zöllner, C. & Stark, R. 2009, 'Investigating three-dimensional sketching for early conceptual design: results from expert discussions and user studies', *Computers & Graphics*, vol. 33, no. 4, pp. 462–473.

Johnson, D., Gardner, J. & Sweetser, P. 2016, 'Motivations for videogame play: predictors of time spent playing', *Computers in Human Behavior*, vol. 63, pp. 805–812.

Jonson, B. 2005, 'Design ideation: the conceptual sketch in the digital age', *Design Studies*, vol. 26, no. 6, pp. 613–624.

Jung, Y. & Joo, M. 2011, 'Building information modelling (BIM) framework for practical implementation', *Automation in Construction*, vol. 20, no. 2, pp. 126–133.

Kim, J.I., Kim, J., Fischer, M. & Orr, R. 2015, 'BIM-based decision-support method for master planning of sustainable large-scale developments', *Automation in Construction*, vol. 58, pp. 95–108.

Kokotovich, V. & Dorst, K. 2016, 'The art of "stepping back": studying levels of abstraction in a diverse design team', *Design Studies*, vol. 46, pp. 79–94.

Kourtit, K., Nijkamp, P. & Stough, R. 2017, 'Foreword: digital support tools for smart cities', *Socio-economic Planning Sciences*, vol. 58, pp. 1–2.

Koutamanis, A. 1993, 'The future of visual design representations in architecture', *Automation in Construction*, vol. 2, no. 1, pp. 47–56.

Kristensen, E.K. 2011, *Systemic barriers to a transformation of the building industry from a buyer controlled to a seller driven industry*, PhD thesis, Robert Gordon University.

Laing, R., Conniff, A., Craig, T., Scott, S. & Galan Diaz, C. 2007, 'Design and use of a virtual heritage model to enable a comparison of active navigation of buildings and spaces with passive observation', *Automation in Construction*, vol. 16, no. 6, pp. 830–841.

Laing, R., Davies, A., Miller, D., Conniff, A., Scott, S. & Morrice, J. 2008, 'The application of visual environmental economics in the study of public preference and urban greenspace', *Environment and Planning B: Planning and Design*, vol. 36, no. 2, pp. 355–375.

Laing, R., Miller, D., Davies, A. & Scott, S. 2006, 'Urban greenspace: the incorporation of environmental values in a decision support system', *IT in Construction*, vol. 11, pp. 177–196.

Lambers, K., Eisenbeiss, H., Sauerbier, M., Kupferschmidt, D., Gaisecker, T., Sotoodeh, S. & Hanusch, T. 2007, 'Combining photogrammetry and laser scanning for the recording and modelling of the Late Intermediate Period site of Pinchango Alto, Palpa, Peru', *Journal of Archaeological Science*, vol. 34, no. 10, pp. 1702–1712.

Lasseter, J. 1987, 'Principles of traditional animation applied to 3D computer animation', in *SIGGRAPH '87 proceedings of the 14th annual conference on computer graphics and interactive techniques*, ACM, New York, pp. 35–44.

Latham, M. 1994, *Constructing the team: the final report of the government/industry review of procurement and contractual arrangements in the UK construction industry*, HMSO, London, UK.

Lawrence, R.J. 1982, 'Trends in architectural design methods: the "liability" of public participation', *Design Studies*, vol. 3, no. 2, pp. 97–103.

Lawrence, R.J. 1983, 'Laypeople as architectural designers', *Leonardo*, vol. 16, no. 3, pp. 232–236.

Lawrence, R.J. 1993, 'Architectural design tools: simulation, communication and negotiation', *Design Studies*, vol. 14, no. 3, pp. 299–313.

Leon, M., Laing, R., Malins, J. & Salman, H. 2014, 'Development and testing of a design protocol for computer mediated multidisciplinary collaboration during the concept stages with application to the built environment', *Procedia Environmental Sciences*, vol. 22, pp. 108–119.

References

Leslie, C. 2017, *Disappearing Glasgow: a photographic journey*, Freight Books, Glasgow.

Lim, S., Qin, S., Prieto, P., Wright, D. & Shackleton, J. 2004, 'A study of sketching behaviour to support free-form surface modelling from on-line sketching', *Design Studies*, vol. 25, no. 4, pp. 393–413.

Liu, Y., van Nederveen, S. & Hertogh, M. 2017, 'Understanding effects of BIM on collaborative design and construction: an empirical study in China', *International Journal of Project Management*, vol. 35, no. 4, pp. 686–698.

Lu, T., Tai, C., Su, F. & Cai, S. 2005, 'A new recognition model for electronic architectural drawings', *Computer-Aided Design*, vol. 37, no. 10, pp. 1053–1069.

Magritte, R. 1928, *The Treachery of Images* [painting].

Mambretti, I.M. 2007, *Urban parks between safety and aesthetics: exploring urban green space using visualisation and conjoint analysis methods*, PhD thesis, ETHz (Swiss Federal Institute of Technology in Zurich).

Mark, E., Martens, B. & Oxman, R. 2003, 'Preliminary stages of CAAD education', *Automation in Construction*, vol. 12, no. 6, pp. 661–670.

Merschbrock, C. 2012, 'Unorchestrated symphony: the case of inter-organizational collaboration in digital construction design', *ITcon*, vol. 17, pp. 333–350.

Merschbrock, C. & Munkvold, B.E. 2015, 'Effective digital collaboration in the construction industry: a case study of BIM deployment in a hospital construction project', *Computers in Industry*, vol. 73, pp. 1–7.

Miguel, M., Laing, R. & Zaman, Q. 2016, 'Explorations of an urban intervention management system: a reflection on how to deal with urban complex systems and deliver dynamic change', in *Digital futures and the city of today: new technologies and physical spaces*, eds. G.A. Caldwell, C. Smith & E. Clift, Intellect Ltd, Bristol.

Mitchell, W.J. 1994, 'Three paradigms for computer-aided design', *Automation in Construction*, vol. 3, no. 2, pp. 239–245.

Mori, M. 1970, 'The uncanny valley', *Energy*, vol. 7, no. 4, pp. 33–35.

Norberg-Schulz, C. 1980, *Genius loci: towards a phenomenology of architecture*, Rizzoli, New York.

Núñez Andrés, A., Buill Pozuelo, F., Regot Marimón, J. & de Mesa Gisbert, A. 2012, 'Generation of virtual models of cultural heritage', *Journal of Cultural Heritage*, vol. 13, no. 1, pp. 103–106.

Oh, M., Lee, J., Hong, S.W. & Jeong, Y. 2015, 'Integrated system for BIM-based collaborative design', *Automation in Construction*, vol. 58, pp. 196–206.

Ohyama, S., Nishiike, S., Watanabe, H., Matsuoka, K., Akizuki, H., Takeda, N. & Harada, T. 2007, 'Autonomic responses during motion sickness induced by virtual reality', *Auris Nasus Larynx*, vol. 34, no. 3, pp. 303–306.

Osman, H.M., Georgy, M.E. & Ibrahim, M.E. 2003, 'A hybrid CAD-based construction site layout planning system using genetic algorithms', *Automation in Construction*, vol. 12, no. 6, pp. 749–764.

Pahl, G., Badke-Schaub, P. & Frankenberger, E. 1999, 'Résumé of 12 years interdisciplinary empirical studies of engineering design in Germany', *Design Studies*, vol. 20, no. 5, pp. 481–494.

Pektaş, Ş.T. 2015, 'The virtual design studio on the cloud: a blended and distributed approach for technology-mediated design education', *Architectural Science Review*, vol. 58, no. 3, pp. 255–265.

Peng, C., Chang, D.C., Blundell Jones, P. & Lawson, B. 2002a, 'Exploring urban history and space online: design of the virtual Sheffield application', *Design Studies*, vol. 23, no. 5, pp. 437–453.

Peng, C., Chang, D.C., Blundell Jones, P. & Lawson, B. 2002b, 'On an alternative framework for building virtual cities: supporting urban contextual modelling on demand', *Environment and Planning B: Urban Analytics and City Science*, vol. 29, no. 1, pp. 87–103.

Penn, A. & Al Sayed, K. 2017, 'Spatial information models as the backbone of smart infrastructure', *Environment and Planning B: Urban Analytics and City Science*, vol. 44, no. 2, pp. 197–203.

Pickford, L. 2015, '10 things facilities managers should know about BIM', RICS website, www.rics.org/uk/news/news-insight/comment/10-things-facilities-managers-should-know-about-bim/, accessed 27 July 2017.

Purcell, P. 1980, 'Computer education in architecture', *Computer-Aided Design*, vol. 12, no. 5, pp. 239–251.

Rattray, C. 2003, 'Doubleness', *Architectural Research Quarterly*, vol. 7, no. 2, pp. 188–192.

Rohrmann, B. & Bishop, I. 2002, 'Subjective responses to computer simulations of urban environments', *Journal of Environmental Psychology*, vol. 22, pp. 319–331.

Sanoff, H. 2011, 'Multiple views of participatory design', *Focus*, vol. 8, no. 1, pp. 11–21.

Scheer, D.R. 2014, *The death of drawing: architecture in the age of simulation*, Routledge, London.

Schenk, P. 1997, 'The role of drawing in graphic design and the implications for curriculum planning', *Journal of Art & Design Education*, vol. 16, no. 1, pp. 73–82.

Schön, D.A. 1983, *The reflective practitioner: how professionals think in action*, Basic Books, New York.

References

Schumann, J., Strothotte, T., Raab, A. & Laser, S. 1996, 'Assessing the effect of non-photorealistic rendered images in CAD', *CHI 1996: proceedings of the SIGCHI Conference on Human Factors in Computing Systems*, pp. 35–41, DOI: 10.1145/238386.238398.

Sener, B. & Wormald, P. 2008, 'User evaluation of HCI concepts for defining product form', *Design Studies*, vol. 29, no. 1, pp. 12–29.

Spence, R. 2007, *Information visualization: design for interaction*, 2nd edn, Pearson Education Limited, Harlow.

Stompff, G., Smulders, F. & Henze, L. 2016, 'Surprises are the benefits: reframing in multidisciplinary design teams', *Design Studies*, vol. 47, pp. 187–214.

Succar, B. 2009, 'Building information modelling framework: a research and delivery foundation for industry stakeholders', *Automation in Construction*, vol. 18, pp. 357–375.

Suwa, M. & Tversky, B. 1997, 'What do architects and students perceive in their design sketches? A protocol analysis', *Design Studies*, vol. 18, no. 4, pp. 385–403.

Themistocleous, K. 2017, 'Model reconstruction for 3D visualization of cultural heritage sites using open data from social media: the case study of Soli, Cyprus', *Journal of Archaeological Science: Reports*, vol. 14, pp. 774–781.

Till, J. 2009, *Architecture depends*, MIT Press, Cambridge, MA.

Tovey, M. 1989, 'Drawing and CAD in industrial design', *Design Studies*, vol. 10, no. 1, pp. 24–39.

Tufte, E. 2001, *The visual display of quantitative information*, 2nd edn, Graphics Press, Cheshire, CT.

Valero, E., Bosché, F., Forster, A., Wilson, L. & Leslie, A. 2017, 'Evaluation of historic masonry: towards greater objectivity and efficiency', in *Heritage Building Information Modelling*, eds. Y. Arayici, J. Counsell, L. Mahdjoubi, G. Nagy, S. Hawas & K. Dewidar, Routledge, London.

Van der Lugt, R. 2005, 'How sketching can affect the idea generation process in design group meetings', *Design Studies*, vol. 26, no. 2, pp. 101–122.

Vesely, D. 2004, *Architecture in the age of divided representation: the question of creativity in the shadow of production*, MIT Press, Cambridge, MA.

Webber, S.S. 2008, 'Development of cognitive and affective trust in teams', *Small Group Research*, vol. 39, no. 6, pp. 746–769.

Whyte, A. 1999, *Building design team communication: practice and education*, PhD thesis, Robert Gordon University.

Willey, D.S. 1976, 'Approaches to computer-aided architectural sketch design', *Computer Aided Design*, vol. 8, no. 3, pp. 181–186.

Wojtowicz, J. 1995, *Virtual design studio*, Hong Kong University Press, Hong Kong.

Yastikli, N. 2007, 'Documentation of cultural heritage using digital photogrammetry and laser scanning', *Journal of Cultural Heritage*, vol. 8, no. 4, pp. 423–427.

Yilmaz, H.M., Yakar, M. & Yildiz, F. 2008, 'Documentation of historical caravansaries by digital close range photogrammetry', *Automation in Construction*, vol. 17, no. 4, pp. 489–498.

Index

123D 107
3D 7–8, 17, 26, 36, 39, 43, 122; collaboration 50, 86, 100, 107; democracy 55, 60–1, 65–6; printing 25, 31–2, 55, 70
3D Studio 41, 103–4
3DS Max 60

abandoned architecture 6, 57, 63
Aberdeen 64, 94–7, 100, 108
abstraction 64, 100
access rights 113
accessibility 8, 110; collaborative 90, 94–5, 97; democratic 55–9, 62
aesthetics 29–30, 38, 42–5, 93, 126–7
Anderson, L. 100
Andrew, C. 82
animation 29
Arniani, M. 68–9
Arnstein, S.R. 4–5, 8, 63, 66–7
augmented reality *see* virtual and augmented reality

Baletti, C. 70
Baxter, S. 86
Beck, H. 14–16
behaviourism 77–9
best practice 53
big data 113
Bilda, Z. 34
block modelling 64
Broadbent, G. 78–9
BSI 112–13, 115–16
building, architecture as 35
building information modelling (BIM) 17–21, 41, 122–31; collaboration 46–9, 53, 73–7; democratic 55, 60, 62; design team 27–8; greenspace 94–5; introduction 3, 5, 8–9; smart cities 113–14, 116

built heritage *see* heritage
Bustillo, A. 40

CAAD 17–19, 21–4, 35–7, 41
CAD/CAM 23, 25–6, 34
Calgary 66–8
Canada 66
capacity 74–5
Carver, S. 66
CDM Regulations 27
Chen, C. 38, 40, 42–3
choice experiments 88
cholera 13
cities 112; modelling 64–6; smart 67, 111–17, 120–1, 127
citizens 115–16, *see also* ladder of citizen participation
climate change 69
cloud computing 38, 60
collaboration 1–5, 8–11, 28, 46, 73–7, 107, 129; digital studio 47–9; future 110, 116; ideas generation 52–4; online/distant communication 49–51; visualisation 17–21
collective awareness platforms (CAPS) 68
collectivists 78–9
communication 26, 40–2, 45–7, 76, 81; drawing as tool 30–5; online/distant 49–51
community 5, 50–1, 59–62, 68, 71, 88, 91
complexity 100–1
Computer-Aided Architectural Design *see* CAAD
conservation 81–3, 99
construction industry 5, 12–13, 19–21, 62, 98, 129; future 121, 123–7; ideas generation 52–3
consultation 4, 62–6, 125
contingent valuation 83, 86, 88
Copenhagen 60

143

Index

cost 55–9, 61, 99, 126
Craig, T. 96
creativity 26
crowd sourcing 67–8, 121
Cullen, G. 100, 103, 120

data 3–5, 17, 20, 123–31; collaboration 53–4, 76, 99; democratic visualisation 55–62, 64, 66–8; education 38–9; smart cities 111, 113–17, 120–1; usability 41–5
data drops 124
Davies, A. 90–1
decision making 6, 73, 116; democratic 63–4, 66, 68–9
democratisation 6–8, 61–70, 80, 107
design team 4, 21, 27–8, 35, 43, 62, 71; collaboration 48–56, 73–7, 79; future 109–10
determinism 78–9
digital architecture 7–8
Digital Design Studio 63
digital studio 37–40, 47–9
digital technologies 1–3, 6–11, 16–21, 32–3, 109; collaboration 49–54; democratic access to 61–70; drawing interfaces 24–7; early uses 21–4; mobile 68, 79, 120; resistance to 29–30; as Trojan Horse 107–8
discovery 24
Dossick, C.S. 76
'Double House' 32
drawing and sketching 2–4, 17–18, 127, 130; collaboration 49–51, 79–80; democratic 60–1, 69–70; as design/communication tool 30–5; early digitisation 21–4; importance of 29–30; interfaces 24–7
drones 63

Eadie, R. 124
Eastman, C.M. 21–3, 36
eCAADe 35–6
economics, environmental 83, 91, 93, 117, 120
Edinburgh 94
education and learning 33–40, 77–80, 110
efficacy, personal 68–9
Elgin 105–7
end user 2, 4, 52–3, 71, 78–9, 109–10, 132
engagement 6, 128, 132; collaboration 76, 78–81, 89, 92, 99, 105; democratic 56, 60–2, 66–8, 71
engineering 14, 41
environment 114–15

environmental economics 83, 91, 93, 117, 120
environmental psychology 78, 109
étalier 49
ETH Zurich 95
Europe 91, 112, 121, 131
European Commission 68–9
experience 77–8

facilities management 120, 122, 124–7
Faeroe Islands 100–2
feedback 17, 66, 73, 120–1
focus groups 71, 89, 91

gaming 103–5, 111, 122–6
geographical information systems (GIS) 45, 66, 86, 91, 94–5
Gero, J.S. 34
Glasgow 63–4
Gothenburg 65–8
GPS 120
graphic design 32
greenspaces 91–6, 126
grit 100–1
group participation 28

heritage 81, 98–101, 125; democracy 57, 59–61, 64, 70–1; marketing 104–7
Hertogh, M. 74
human–computer interface (HCI) 12, 22, 40–1
Hunter, A.J.S. 66–7
Hutton Institute 94
Hyde, R. 24

ideas generation 52–4
image manipulation 81–3, 125
image sorting 96–7
immersive reality *see* virtual and augmented reality
industrialisation 20, 22–3
information *see* building information modelling (BIM); data
informing the public 4
infrastructure 116–17
insight 11–12
integration. 19
Internet 6, 8, 34, 37, 48, 51, 114; collaboration 81, 83, 90–2; democracy 57, 62, 65–8, 71
Internet of things (IoT) 113
interworking 114–15
Isikdag, U. 125

Jonson, B. 33
Jung, Y. 20

144

Index

keystoning 84–5
knowledge 20; prior 42

ladder of citizen participation 4–5, 8, 63–4, 67, 128, 132
Laing, R. 40
laser scanning 107, 131; democracy 56–7, 59–60, 63–4, 70; future 111, 128; heritage 98–9
Lawrence, R.J. 30, 78
leadership 77
learning and education 33–40, 77–80, 110
life cycle 17, 23; aesthetics 43, 45; future 121, 123, 125–6
Liu, Y. 74
local authorities 62–4, 117
London 13–16, 95, 123

Magritte, R. 99
Mambretti, I.M. 95–6
management 12, 53–4, 74–5; facilities/estates 120, 122, 124–7
maps 12–16
Mark, E. 36
marketing 6, 100–7
markets 112
Merschbrock, C. 74–5
metadata 116
methods 56–61, 78, 83, 89, 91–2
Mexico 79
Miller, D. 94
'Min Stad' 65–6
Minard, C.J. 12
Minecraft 122
Mitchell, W.J. 48–9
mobile technology 68, 79, 120
mobility 113, 121, *see also* transport
modelling 17–21, 27–32, 34–5, 131; collaboration 86, 96, 100–8; democratic access 55–6, 61–70; introduction 3, 6–8; methods 56–60; in practice 47–50; usability 40–5
Moscow 12
municipal authorities *see* local authorities
Munkvold, B.E. 74

Napoleon 12
nD modelling 45, 131
Neff, G. 76
Newcastle 63–4
Northumbria University 63

Occulus Rift 105
Oh, M. 75
open access 62

open source 56, 103, 114
Ordnance Survey 88
ownership 125–6
Oxman, R. 36

paradigms 48–9
parks 91–6, 126
Pektaş, Ş.T. 37–8
personal efficacy 68–9
perspective 57, 104
phenomenology 78–9, 103
photogrammetry 40, 57–61, 63–4, 70, 128, 131
photography 82–3, 104; image sorting 96–7; tilt shift 57–9, 82
Photoshop 104
Pickford, L. 124
placation 4–5
planning 62–7, 78, 80, 115; spatial 22
plans 17
plants 95
policy 8–9
post-occupancy evaluation (POE) 124
practice 5, 8–10, 19–22, 47–54, 110, 129–32; education 36–8
printing: 3D 25, 31–2, 55, 70; images 83
prior knowledge 42
private finance initiative (PFI) 125
procurement 5
programming 36
prototyping 23, 32
psychology, environmental 78, 109
public *see* consultation; transport
Purcell, T. 34, 36

quantity surveyors 50, 53–4

rating 91
realism 42, 132
reference data 117
relationships, interpersonal 76–7
representation 22
RICS 123
rights 113

scale 125
scanning *see* laser scanning
scenarios 89, 92
Scheer, D.R. 47
Schenk, P. 32
Schön, D.A. 37
Scotland 81, 86, 94–5, 100, 105–7, 114
sensors 68, 117, 120
Silk Road 61
simulation 35, 38, 41, 49, 126

145

sketching *see* drawing and sketching
smart cities 67, 111–17, 120–1, 127
Snow, J. 11, 13, 95
social media 66, 68
soft landings 123, 126
software 1, 5, 21–3, 86, 114; collaboration 50, 73–4, 77; democratic access to 60–1; final remarks 129–31; in marketing 103–5; usability 40–2
spatial planning 22
Spence, R. 12–13
Standard Method of Measurement (SMM7) 3
standards 19–20
stereo photogrammetry 60
streetscapes 86–9
studio, digital/virtual 38–40, 47–9
Succar, B. 19–21
surveying 50, 53–4, 59, 70, 98
surveys 92
sustainability 68, 112
Sweden 65–6
synthetic team 79

tablets 25, 111
Tait, E. 107
technology *see* digital technology
text 93–4
thematic data 117
Till, J. 26–7
tilt shift photography 57–9, 82
time, freezing 27
Tinganes 102
Tonge, K. 82
tools, purpose 30
training 74, 124
transport 14–16, 95, 113, 115–17, 121
trees 95
trust 76

UK 3, 27, 63–4, 71, 115, 123
underground map 14–16
Underwood, J. 125
urbanisation 112
USA 21
usability 40–2
user 109–10, *see also* end user; engagement

Valero, E. 60–1
value 83, 86, 117, 120
Van der Lugt, R. 32–3
van Nederveen, S. 74
Vesely, D. 26
virtual and augmented reality 79, 110–11, 120–1, 127
virtual studio 38–40, 47–9
visualisation 11–13, 16–17, 41–6, 67, 132; drawing interfaces 25–6; in education 35–40; future directions 111, 126; greenspace 91–6; heritage studies 99–101; image manipulation 80–3; image sorting 96–7; introduction 2, 6–7; in marketing 101–7; online rating 86–91

walk-throughs 101, 105
water 13
weather 29, 101–2
Webber, S.S. 76
Whyte, A. 28
Willey, D.S. 23
Woolf Architects 32
workflows 14, 24, 64, 75–6, 99, 130

Yastikli, N. 60
Young, M. 82

Zurich 95, 108

PGMO 12/05/2018